Culture and Conflict in the Middle East

Culture and Conflict in the Middle East

Philip Carl Salzman

Humanity Books

an imprint of Prometheus Books
59 John Glenn Drive, Amherst, New York 14228-2119

Published 2008 by Humanity Books, an imprint of Prometheus Books

Inquiries should be addressed to
Humanity Books
59 John Glenn Drive
Amherst, New York 14228–2119
VOICE: 716–691–0133, ext. 210
FAX: 716–691–0137

12 11 10 09 08   5 4 3 2

Library of Congress Cataloging-in-Publication Data

Salzman, Philip Carl.
    Culture and conflict in the Middle East / Philip Carl Salzman.
        p. cm.
    Includes bibliographical references and index.
    ISBN 978-1-59102-587-0
    1. Middle East—Civilization. 2. Middle East—Social conditions.
3. Conflict management—Middle East. 4. National security—Middle East.
I. Title.

DS57.S286 2008
303.60956—dc22

                                                    2007046895

Printed in the United States of America on acid-free paper

Dedicated to Ernest Gellner

CONTENTS

Chapter 1

INTRODUCTION

"Men and societies frequently treat the institutions and assumptions by which they live as absolute, self-evident, and given."
Ernest Gellner, *Plough, Sword and Book,* p. 11

Arab culture, the dominant culture of the central Middle East and the founding culture of Islam, is both a brilliant construction of human creativity and a practical response to many human problems. Like all cultures, it opens some paths and closes others. In other words, Arab culture, like every other culture, solves some problems and opens some possibilities, while presenting problems of its own and limiting other possibilities. This book explores the contours and consequences, both liberating and restricting, of Arab culture, as an opening into Middle Eastern life.

Arab culture, like all cultures, is a way of construing the

world, the universe, society, and men and women. It is, at the same time, a matrix of meaning, a framework for understanding, and a plan for action. It defines desirable goals, appropriate means, and the broader values to be honored in human action. By so doing, Arab culture is a force in human action, a sculptor of society, a major influence on human events. Arab culture is a potent force, but not the only one, for human life is shaped by multiple influences: internal ones such as biology and psychology, parallel ones such as the laws of sociology and economics, and external ones such as contact with other cultures and societies. However, understanding these other influences without taking into account Arab culture would be insufficient for appreciating the realities of the central Middle East.

Arab culture addresses the universal problem of order and security in an ingenious and time-tested fashion. Every human society must find a way to establish a substantial degree of order and security if it is going to survive and prosper. By order I mean a predictable repetitiveness of behavior, such that members of the society can count on a reliable result for any of their acts. Order is absolutely critical, because without it, people do not know the results of their actions, and so either they do not act, or act arbitrarily, and thus chaos ensues.

For example, if it is not known whether a cultivated crop will be burned, trampled under hoof, or stolen—if people do not know that there is a good chance that they will benefit from the fruits of their labor—they will not bother to plant, and so there will be no cultivation of foodstuffs, medicinals, and raw material crops. If people do not know whether their children will respect them and support them in old age, or will usurp and destroy them at the first opportunity, they will be reluctant to nurture them and keep them close. If people do not know whether strangers, coming to their community, will respect their lives and property, or whether they will attack and loot them, they will be loath to welcome strangers at all, and strive to drive away anyone who approaches.

Security is confidence that persons, rights, and property—however defined in a particular culture—will be respected. Every culture defines norms, or rules of correct behavior, about persons, rights, and property, and validates a set of social arrangements to guarantee that these are respected. Social arrangements to guarantee security can be referred to as the organization of social control. Arab culture in the central Middle East is characterized by a particular form of social control that has a major impact on human experience and social life. This form, or structure, is what I will call "balanced opposition."

Balanced opposition is an ingenious way to organize security. It is decentralized, in that no central officials or organizers are required. It is democratic, in that decision making is collective and everyone has a say. It is egalitarian, in that there is no ascribed status, rank, or hierarchy into which people are born, and all groups and individuals are equal in principle. It is also to a substantial degree effective, in that balanced opposition often successfully deters attack by threatening reprisal.

This is how balanced opposition in the Middle East works: Everybody is a member of a nested set of kin groups, from very small to very large. These groups are vested with responsibility for the defense of each and every one of its members and responsibility for the harm each and every one of its members do to outsiders. This is called by anthropologists "collective responsibility," and the actions taken by a group on its own behalf are called "self-help." If there is a confrontation, small groups face opposing small groups, middle-sized groups face opposing middle-sized groups, or large groups face opposing large groups: family vs. family, lineage vs. lineage, clan vs. clan, tribe vs. tribe, confederacy vs. confederacy, sect vs. sect, the Islamic community (*umma*) vs. the infidels. This is where the deterrence lies, in the balance between opponents; individuals do not face groups, and small groups do not face large groups. Any potential aggressor knows that his target is not solitary or meager, but is always, in principle, a formidable formation much the same size as his.

There is also an internal group aspect to this deterrence. Because of the collective responsibility, in which all members of a group are responsible for each other, each member of the group is implicated in the actions of every other member. This means that all group members may be called to fight in order to defend a member in a conflict, or to seek vengeance in the case of loss of property, injury, or death, or to pay compensation in the case of a group member causing injury to another, or would be a legitimate target for a member of the opposing group. But of course many individual group members would much rather avoid being dragged into fights or payments by the arrogant assertions, irrational passions, or rash adventures of their fellow group members. So these group members put pressure on other group members to behave cautiously and prudently, and to avoid pursuing opportunities to enter into conflict. Here is the internal deterrence: the pressure and even threat of withdrawal of support of fellow group members. It is common, for example, for older men to urge caution upon the young men who tend to have quicker tempers, and for those group members somewhat more distant in kinship from those directly involved in the conflict to urge prudence upon the close kin, who would feel the insult, injury, or loss more strongly.

Balanced opposition works to the extent that it does because individual members of groups come to the aid of their fellow group members, even at serious risk of injury or loss of life, or with serious material cost. Why do they do this? For two main reasons: one pragmatic, the other cultural. The pragmatic reason is the strong belief that the only ones who can be counted on for help are members of one's kinship group. You act to support your fellow members, on the understanding that they will come to your aid when you are in need. This is what anthropologists call "generalized reciprocity," in which you act now to support group members, in the expectation that, some time later, when needed, they will support you. This is sensible self-interest. The cultural reason is that your honor depends upon your living up to your commitments, in this case as a member of the group. If you are not willing to set aside your short-term personal interest, your comfort, and safety to come to the aid of your fellow members, you lose your honor and standing, earn a bad reputation, are not respected by others, and are avoided as a partner in any enterprise.

Balanced opposition, a decentralized system of defense and social control characterized by self-help, is a "tribal" form of organization. Tribes operate quite differently from states, which are centralized, have political hierarchies, and have specialized institutions—such as courts, police, and an army, with tax collectors providing the means for support—to maintain social control and defense. Preindustrial states are best thought of as centers of military power that claimed control over a wide territory and its population, but that in reality waxed and waned over time in their effective reach. Their ambitions seldom went beyond collecting taxes and defending taxpayers from other predators. While tribes tend to operate democratically, states, until modern times, have tended to rule tyrannically. Those who governed states did so in their own interest, and usually at the expense of the general populace. Thus states expanded whenever possible, bringing in more loot for the rulers and their followers, more bodies for their armies, and more peasants to tax. Members of tribal societies understandably resisted being incorporated into states, preferring their independent and egalitarian communal lives to exploitation by an arrogant and brutal elite. "Tribal" is thus used here primarily in a descriptive sense. If any evaluation were intended, it would not be disparaging, for it is not difficult to prefer independence to oppression, equality to hierarchy, and self-help to suppression.

The remarkable development of Islam in the seventh century CE must be understood, to a degree, within the context of Arabian balanced opposition. Islam provided in the *umma* (the community of Muslims) a more inclusive level of integration than tribal organization. But at the same time, it also provided an opponent to the *umma*: the world of infidels, which had to be confronted for the glory of God and for the profit of plunder (deemed as already belonging to Muslims). Islam, whatever its many dimensions and complexities were, incorporated the balanced opposition structure of the tribal society which it overlay. Perhaps it could hardly have done otherwise and been accepted as it was.

The thesis of this book is that balanced opposition is a dominant theme in Arab culture and a central structure in Arab society. Furthermore, as I shall argue shortly, balanced opposition shapes other aspects of social life and, like all structures, limits the possibilities. Is this thesis open to the criticism widespread in postmodern and postcolonial theory that characterizing societies is a form of essentializing distortion, assuming uniformity and denying the humanity of the members of the society?

The postcolonial argument set forth in Edward Said's groundbreaking *Orientalism* (1978), that people are really more or less the same, and that any distinctions between cultures impose a false essentialism aimed at defining certain populations as "other" primarily to demean them and justify imperial and colonial oppression, rashly dismissed culture as of nugatory significance. The assumption that all people are just like "us" is a kind of ethnocentrism that projects our values, our ways of thinking, and our goals onto other peoples. The anthropological study of culture around the world is based on a recognition of cultural differences, on an appreciation of the importance of culture in people's lives, and on respect for other people's cultures.

The postcolonial argument that knowledge of other cultures is impossible because people and cultures do not exhibit uniformity jumps from a known fact to a false inference. All knowledge is based on abstraction, and abstraction draws commonalities and averages that exist beyond the acknowledged variation of the particulars. For example, there are different species and varieties of camel, but we would not therefore conclude that we cannot validly distinguish camels from horses. Tents too are different from one another, in materials used and in structure; yet tents are not houses, and the differences are fairly obvious. As regards cultures, there are variations both between and within Arab and Middle Eastern cultures, but anyone who argues on that basis that it is impossible to distinguish Arab culture from Hindu culture would not be being frank.

It is clear to me, and I believe any serious anthropologist would agree (see Lindholm 2002: 6), that we can successfully study Arab and Middle Eastern society and establish sound knowledge of it. In that knowledge, an understanding of balanced opposition would play a major role.

Describing a central institution of the Arab world is worthwhile in its own right. But my interest, and the intent of this book, is to go beyond ethnographic description to social-anthropological explanation. The purpose of this book is to describe both the presence and importance of balanced opposition in the Arab world, and the consequences of balanced opposition for other aspects of Arab society and culture.

One important consequence of reliance on balanced opposition is an emphasis on individual independence, freedom, and responsibility, and also on equality and democracy. At the same time, the military virtues of prowess and courage, and the goal of domination, are highly valued. The reasons for this are clear. A decentralized system of defense based upon self-help, such as balanced opposition, relies on each individual to make judgments and act on his own or freely in collaboration with his fellow groups members. Acting in defense and retaliation means engaging in violence, for which skill and courage are desirable. In tribal societies based on balanced opposition, male children are raised to be independent, to take responsibility for themselves, and to be ready and able to engage in sanctioned violence against designated enemies. Collective decisions about action are made democratically in councils in which all group members are free to speak. No mechanisms of coercion are available to force group members to act. Collective agreement on decisions puts moral pressure on each individual to fulfill his duty, and his reputation and honor are at stake. But ultimately it is up to each individual to decide and act. The honorable man has no ruler and bows to no man, but stands on his own feet and his own reputation as an equal to all others.

Thus adherence to balanced opposition results in individual and group independence, freedom, responsibility, equality, bellicosity, and courage. At the same time, however, balanced opposition is a frame that limits alternatives, some of which might have proven useful. Balanced opposition emphasizes particular loyalties: my lineage against the other lineage; my tribal section against the other tribal section; my tribe against the other tribe; Muslims against infidels. This particularism of loyalties is not consistent with a universalistic normative frame, for example, a constitution of rules which is inclusive, applying equally to everyone. Balanced opposition is rule by group loyalty, rather than rule by rules. Factionalism is the norm; there is a constant fission into smaller groups in opposition to one another, and fusion into larger groups opposed to one another. This structural contingency too is inconsistent with constitutional rule in which rules apply to all and are upheld by all at all times. Particularism and contingency, so basic to complementary opposition, preclude universalistic constitutional frameworks and thus inhibit social and political integration at broader territorial levels including larger and diverse populations.

The cultural frame of complementary opposition in the Middle East thus underlies many of the difficulties in building a civil society, establishing democracy at the state level, maintaining public support for state institutions, founding creative educational institutions, inspiring economic development, and building an inclusive public culture in the Middle East. Now it is not the job of anthropologists to laud societies or to criticize them, to celebrate or to demean them. So problems and difficulties are a very delicate matter to address, even more when they appear to be culturally driven. No anthropologist wants to appear to be disparaging the people and culture that he or she is studying and discussing.

However, the problems and difficulties of the Arab Middle East are a matter of public record. Furthermore, and perhaps most usefully for anthropologists, they are a matter of discussion among Middle Eastern Arabs themselves. In other words, criticism is part of a contemporary, intracultural debate, and is thus part of contemporary Arab culture. Drawing on this debate would appear to be unexceptionable, even for an anthropologist, as long as the positions identified are understood as contested.

As already indicated, the thesis of this book is that social and cultural patterns that I label "balanced opposition," which have been so serviceable for Arab Middle Easterners and so important in their history, also impose constraints that inhibit developments in the Middle East that are advocated by some Middle Easterners themselves, and deemed desirable by some external observers as well.

This is how we shall proceed: I shall begin by looking at

balanced opposition in its social context, and then explore its limitations and problems. In chapter 2, "Making a Living in the Middle East: Life in the Valleys, Deserts, and Mountains," we review the basic facts of material life and social relations in the historical and in much of the contemporary Middle East. Chapter 3, "Friends and Enemies: Security and Defense in the Middle East," examines our main exploratory focus, that major pattern in Middle Eastern culture, the social principle of balanced opposition. In chapter 4, "Defense and Offense: Honor and Rank in the Middle East," we see how the notion of "honor" reinforces lineage organization, and how competition for honor results in an esteem-ranking hierarchy. Chapter 5, "Turning toward the World: Tribal Organization and Predatory Expansion," addresses the way in which balanced opposition has shaped external relations, relations with other peoples. In chapter 6, "Tribe and State: The Dynamics of Incompatibility," we explore some of the strengths and weaknesses of contemporary Middle Eastern societies, and their foundations. Finally, in chapter 7, "Root Causes: The Middle East Today and Tomorrow," I turn to some prominent interpretations of the Middle East and argue that our analysis both fits with and enhances them.

In exploring culture and conflict in the Middle East, focusing on tribal culture, I draw on the excellent accounts of Arab tribal life written by anthropologists. In their roles as ethnographic fieldworkers, these anthropologists have lived, often for years, among Arab and neighboring tribal peoples, spoken with them in their Arabic or other local dialect, and recorded their beliefs and practices. Their reports are foundation blocks of this book.

As well, in constructing the argument of this work, and in providing illustrations, I also draw on my own research among a nomadic, tribal people in Iranian Baluchistan, across the Persian Gulf from Arabia. The Iranian-speaking tribes of the highland Sarhad region of Baluchistan have an organizational structure like that of the Bedouin. I have reported on these Baluchi tribes in a series of articles, but above all in *Black Tents of Baluchistan*. They are desert dwellers like the Bedouin, and relevant for this work because they depend upon balanced opposition to order their political relations. Nor are they the only non-Arab tribal peoples to rely on balanced opposition as their primary organizational principle. The Turkic-speaking Turkmen of northeastern Iran, on the southwest edge of central Asia, similarly organize their social and political relations around balanced opposition. I refer especially to the Yomut Turkmen described by William Irons in *The Yomut Turkmen*. The Sarhadi tribes and the Turkmen are Muslims like the Bedouin, and predominantly Sunni Muslim. The parallels with the Arab tribes are strong, and I believe that reference to these peoples will prove to be illuminating.

Chapter 2

MAKING A LIVING
IN THE MIDDLE EAST

Life in the Valleys, Deserts, and Mountains

The agricultural revolution was the domestication of natural or "wild" species and their husbanding under human control. Both plants and animals were domesticated and husbanded, but were not always and everywhere susceptible to the same treatment. The division between crop cultivation and animal husbandry was and remains quite marked in the Middle East. To begin with "ideal types," or stereotypes, people specialized in agriculture often are sedentary, live in villages, and are peasants living under state control. People specialized in animal husbandry commonly are nomadic, live in tents, and are tribal, living to a greater or lesser degree independently. Of course life in the Middle East and elsewhere is more complicated than simple dichotomies, and we will explore some of the complications. But there are real tendencies in the Middle East that the dichotomy summarizes.

CLIMATE AND POPULATION

The climate of the Middle East is dominantly tropical arid—that is, hot and dry. To make matters more difficult, the modest precipitation comes in the winter, which means that moisture and warm sun do not coincide, so that the most favorable conditions for cultivation are absent. Because of the climate, cultivation in the Middle East is favored only in limited geographical contexts. The two main ones are river valleys and the higher altitudes of hills and mountains, particularly those facing large bodies of water. River valleys, such as the Nile and Tigris-Euphrates valleys, are especially desirable for cultivation because crops can be watered by irrigation and are not totally dependent upon precipitation. Hills and mountains, such as the coastal range in Cyrenaica on the Libyan coast, facing the Mediterranean, the southern Zagros Mountains of Iran facing the Persian Gulf, the Atlas Mountains of the Maghreb facing the Mediterranean, and the Elburz Mountains facing the Caspian Sea, catch moisture coming off of the water and so have a much higher precipitation than inland areas.

Away from the river valleys and moist flanks, aridity prevails. To the east and west of the Nile Valley are deserts; to the east and west of the Tigris-Euphrates is desert; to the south of the Atlas is the Sahara; to the south of the Elburz is the dry Iranian plateau; to the east of the Zagros is the central desert of Iran. Inland mountains and plateaus, such as those of Arabia and Baluchistan, are unrelentingly arid, gaining relief only from the runoff of melting snow on mountain peaks.

To illustrate this common geographical pattern, let us take as an example Cyrenaica, the eastern half of Libya (Evans-Pritchard 1949). At its northern extent, Cyrenaica forms a rounded peninsula jutting out into the Mediterranean Sea. The northern part of the peninsula takes the form of a large, mountainous plateau, with a broad initial level at 200–500 meters rising to a higher and narrower plateau of 875 meters. This tableland is called in Arabic *al-Jabal al-Akhdar*, "the Green Mountain," after its evergreen forests (Evans-Pritchard 1949: 29). The center of the plateau receives heavy rainfall of 400–550 mm, with a gradual decline to 100 mm at the margins of the tableland (Evans-Pritchard 1949: 30–31). From there begins *al-barr*, the steppe, which sees a rapid decline of rainfall to 50 mm, and then to little or none.

> The plateau slopes southwards through a juniper belt. There forest ends and it continues to roll to the southern steppe in stony undulations dissected by many wadis [water runoff channels, some as large as riverbeds, often dry]. In the plain at its foot there is plenty of grass and low scrub, and vegetation is thick in depression, but the country becomes increasingly desolate the farther to the south one journeys towards the lifeless wastes of the Sahara. . . . The distribution of vegetation in Cyrenaica follows variation in degree of precipitation. Where there is much rain there is forest. Where there is little rain there is steppe. Where there is no rain there is desert. (Evans-Pritchard 1949: 31–33)

In the river valleys and on the moist hilly flanks of the Middle East, we find agricultural villages. Those in the valleys often engage in irrigation double cropping, while those on the flanks relying on precipitation typically grow winter grain crops. In some other areas, such as the dry eastern flanks of the Zagros in Iran, long-distance irrigation tunnels, drawing on water tables at higher elevations, are constructed to make agriculture possible. Elsewhere, in the vast stretches of Saharan, Egyptian, Arabian, and Iranian deserts, cultivation is minor and chancy. There we find a heavy emphasis on the raising of livestock on natural, open range, a practice that anthropologists call "pastoralism" (Salzman 2004).

In Cyrenaica, to continue with our example, the high table-land has been an important agricultural area of settled villages during some periods. In classical times, Cyrenaica was part of Rome and occupied by Roman farming villages. In the first half of the twentieth century, the Italians colonized Cyrenaica and Italians worked farms there. However—and here we begin to see complications in the geographical picture—the Bedouin, who were the main inhabitants of Cyrenaica since a millennium previous when they conquered the Christians, Jews, and pagans who lived there, emphasized pastoralism even on the forested plateau. They adapted to the generous environment of "the Green Mountain" by means of goat and cattle pastoralism.

Even in Cyrenaica, where the distinction between village peasant and nomadic tribesman is negated by the dominance of tribal life, dichotomies are evident: "the mountain and the plain, the forest and the steppe, the red soils and the white, the region of goats and cows and the region of sheep and camels, settled life and nomadism" (Evans-Pritchard 1949: 34).

Evans-Pritchard (1949: 33) attributes the Cyrenaican emphasis on pastoralism among the Bedouin of "the Green Mountain" to "an observed fact that every few years in Cyrenaica there is a year in which the fall of rain is insufficient, or too badly distributed, to raise an adequate crop. In a mixed economy this fact must have given an overwhelming bias towards pastoralism." There may be something in this explanation, but it would not account for why the Romans and Italians emphasized farming, while the Bedouin emphasized pastoralism, with cultivation as a complement. The answer, however, may lie not in geography, but in politics: The farmers were part of and effectively controlled by powerful states; the Bedouin were tribesmen, largely independent of state control. Their nomadism was a political and military tool; maintaining it helped to maintain their independence. Pastoralists can be nomadic; farmers cannot. Even where farming was possible, there were other motives and considerations that biased the Bedouin toward pastoralism. Off of the Cyrenaican Green Mountain, to the south, where rainfall cultivation was impossible, sheep and camel pastoralism was necessarily dominant. Deeper into the Sahara, the land was largely unoccupied, although sometimes crossed by camel herders.

PRODUCTION AND SETTLEMENT

Demography follows climate and productivity. In the river valleys, with water readily available and heavy in nutrients, the land is highly productive and the human population dense. Settlement is characterized by large villages placed closely by one another. On the moist hill and mountain flanks, rainfall determines density. The heavier the rainfall, the higher the agricultural productivity, and the denser the human settlement. In these areas, villages of moderate size tend to be moderate distances from one another.

In the semidesert and desert areas, productivity is low except in those limited areas where long-distance irrigation systems (or recently, mechanized irrigation systems) have been built. Occasional oases, drawing on local water sources, provide nodes of density. But generally the semidesert and desert areas are exploited through extensive means of production using the very limited resources in a wide area. Livestock range widely, consuming the thin grasses and bushes in an area and then moving on to another area. This pastoralism is characterized in the Middle East by a settlement pattern of wide-ranging nomadism, the movement of the local community in the course of the annual round of productive activities. Typically, Middle Eastern nomads dwell in tents woven of black goat hair, and they use camels to transport household goods during migrations.

One variation of the Middle Eastern demographic pattern is nicely illustrated in Yemen, in southwest Arabia, in the region called the Hadramaut. Geographically, this area of southern Yemen consists of two large, desertic, high plateaus, divided by a large valley, fed with water from the wadi system of runoff channels originating on the plateaus. Bujra (1971: 2) describes the population distribution:

> The valley system makes up less than 10 per cent of the total area of the Hadramaut, but it is densely populated and, with 100,000 people, holds about one-third of the estimated total population. Throughout the length of these valleys and their tributaries there are villages and towns scattered with less than a mile from one to the next. . . . The famous 'sky-scraper' towns . . . each with anything from 10,000 to 20,000 people.

What exactly explains the high population density in this region? The average annual rainfall in Yemen is less than two inches, hardly enough to sustain life at all, never mind agriculture and dense agricultural towns. Bujra (1971: 2–3) explains:

> When it rains on the plateau the water flows down the valleys, gathering water from the tributaries and flowing along a well-marked course, more or less in the centre of the valleys. Every village and town then diverts some of this water along a canal and directs it to its own cultivated area. There it is distributed by a complex canal system to every plot and date-palm. The system is a maze of interlocking channels.

Beyond the towns, in the less generously endowed areas of the valley system and on the vast plateaux are found Bedouin thinly scattered in tent camps and hamlets, depending on livestock to make a living.

While villagers specialize in agricultural crops, and nomads specialize in raising livestock, both groups tend to diversify their products as much as possible. They engage in a range of productive activities and hope to benefit from different kinds of products. Villagers do try to raise livestock, even if in small numbers. In some areas they gather wild vegetable species and hunt. Nomads often engage in opportunistic cultivation in such places as water runoff channels, or *wadi*. But in more favored regions, they engage in cultivation systematically. As Evans-Pritchard (1949: 37) says of the Bedouin of Cyrenaica, "Although the Bedouin are by practice and inclination shepherds first and cultivators afterwards, all plough. Barley and some wheat are a staple food. Indeed, in most years they cultivate a surplus of barley which they trade. . . ." Middle Eastern nomads eat bread as a main staple and they must acquire grain to make it. Barley is required as feed for horses. Nomads also search out and collect natural vegetable species, and are often avid hunters. A lucrative sideline is predatory raiding of villages, caravans, and herds. And it is not unusual to offer guard or "protection" services for caravans and oases, which ranges between honest help and extortion.

There are two very good reasons for productive diversification. The first is that many Middle Eastern villagers and nomads are subsistence producers, aiming their products primarily for their own consumption. That being the case, diversification provides a wider range of consumables, which is both less monotonous and more nourishing. Villagers can add to their staples of grain and dates: wild fruits and vegetables, milk products and occasional meat from livestock, and meat from hunting. Nomads can add grain, wild fruits and vegetables, and meat from hunting to the milk products and occasion meat from their livestock, as well as what can be found in or bought from the proceeds of raiding and services.

The other reason is the vulnerability of any particular kind of production to certain substantial variations in climatic conditions or environmental circumstances. For example, if a crop of grain fails because of an unusually low rainfall, or a break-down in the irrigation system, or the arrival of a crop-destroying pest, people must either draw on other kinds of products or else starve. If herds are lost to drought, raiding, or disease, nomads must rely on their cultivation, hunting, and raiding to provide for basic subsistence consumption. Produc-tive diversification thus makes possible flexibility in the face of environmental fluctuations and greater security in providing for human needs.

In Baluchistan, in the rocky deserts of southeastern Iran, the tribesmen of the highland Sarhad region pursue a diversi-fied economy (Salzman 2000). They raise goats, sheep, and camels, and prefer to think of themselves as *wasildar*, herd owners. But they also engage seriously in cultivation, both of date palms and grain crops, the grain with scarce irrigation water, or, more commonly, depending on runoff from hills. Hunting and gathering provide a limited supplement as well. However, these Baluch depend upon external income as another major source for their economy. In the past, up until the 1930s, predatory raiding of distant villages, caravans, and herds was regular and lucrative. Agricultural products, live-stock, manufactured goods such as carpets, and captives to be sold or used as slaves were taken by the Baluchi raiders. Since effective encapsulation by the Iranian state during the mid-twentieth century, these Baluchi tribesmen have replaced raiding with migrant labor, selling their labor on the market in Iran, Pakistan, and, more recently, in the Emirates across the Persian Gulf, and with trading, bringing goods from Pakistan and selling them in Iran. This external income, whatever its source, covers any shortfalls in production at home in Baluchistan.

SUBSISTENCE PRODUCTION AND MARKET PRODUCTION

Middle Eastern cultivators and pastoralists produce food products for their own direct consumption, but not exclusively for that purpose. A considerable amount of what they produce is directed elsewhere. Peasants produce not only for themselves but also for the tax collector and for their landlords, if they have them. From the point of view of state authorities and of landowners, the purpose of the peasantry is to provide them with income. State tax collectors, police, and army are institutional tools used to extract funds and control peasant producers. There is no benevolence in this system of government, merely the strong and well organized extracting from the poorly organized weak. Let us recall that Middle Eastern urban centers had administrative, military, religious, craft, and commercial functions, but produced little and depended upon the rural hinterland for products and material to consume, process, and trade.

Beyond taxes and landlord fees, if further products can be spared from consumption, they can be directed to markets for sale and trade. We must not forget that Middle Eastern markets, bazaars, and suks have been central to Middle Eastern life for thousands of years, and that trade is one of the lifebloods of the region. No apparently benighted peasant scratching at the land of his muddy village, or isolated Bedouin wandering through the desert wastes, is unaware of the current prices of his products in the marketplaces of his region. Indeed, market prices are a staple of Middle Eastern rural conversation.

For example, the Cyrenaican Bedouin, themselves numbering around 150,000 souls, around 30,000 families, exported around 80,000 head of sheep and goats a year, a bit less than three head per family annually, to Egypt in the first quarter of the twentieth century (Evans-Pritchard 1949: 37). As well, they exported large amounts of valuable clarified butter, the figure for 1922 being 91,835 kilos, which was around 3 kilos per family. Animal skins and wool were also sold. Exports were not limited to livestock and livestock products. Cyrenaican grain grown by Bedouin, of a value of 40,000 lire sterling, was exported each year at the end of the nineteenth century and comprised much of the barley bought by English brewers (Evans-Pritchard 1949: 38)! The Bedouin export in order to gain currency that can be used to import products they wish to buy. Staples that must be purchased are tea, sugar, rice, and woolen cloth (Evans-Pritchard 1949: 38).

Let us take one more illustration from the heart of Arabia. The Rwala Bedouin in northern Arabia have traditionally specialized in raising camels (Lancaster 1997). This seems natural to the observer; the Rwala live in the desert and the camel is the best desert livestock. But why raise camels, and why live in the desert? The answer, or at least part of the answer, is that for millennia there has been a strong market demand in the Middle East for camels. Camels have traditionally brought a good price and allowed those who raised them a good living. The reason is that camels were required for the caravan trade, which was such a major part of the Middle Eastern economy. Merchants and traders always required a good supply of camels for their caravans. The solitary Bedouin wandering with his camels in the distant desert wastes, seemingly so disconnected with swarming cities and crass commerce, had in mind the urban livestock market, which was the destination of many of his animals. It was only with the advent of motorized vehicles and their application for commercial transport that camel caravans fell out of use. Faced with this declining market, the Bedouin reluctantly switched to raising sheep, for which the market remained strong (Lancaster 1997: 99).

We must keep in mind that a breeding herd of livestock usually provides a surplus of animals that can be disposed of without harm, and commonly with benefit to the remainder.

A breeding herd consists of a body of fertile females, perhaps 95–98 percent of the adults, and the prelactating young. The postfertile females, and the great bulk of the males, are superfluous. They can be disposed of with no negative impact on the herd, and in fact their absence reduces the competition for pasture, water, and labor. While the pastoralists subsist primarily on grain and milk, the many surplus male sheep, goats, and camels can be sold, depending on the nature of the market, for work, such as transport or traction, or for meat, as can postfertile females. For this reason, livestock production can comfortably be integrated with the marketplace.

SOCIAL RELATIONS

Villagers in the Middle East are commonly peasants, defined by anthropologists as rural primary producers under state control. There are also some pastoral nomads who are peasants. Peasants do not form an independent society, but are a part of a larger society that consists also of urban craftsmen, merchants, religious specialists, and government officials. Peasants meet the rest of society mostly in the form of tax collectors and police or military enforcers, and to some extent junior representatives of the religious establishment. The relation of the state to the peasants is that of the shepherd to his flock: the state fleeces the peasants, making a living off of them, and protects them from other predators, so that they may be fleeced again.

Among themselves, notwithstanding the large villages that they sometime form, peasants tend to be socially fragmented. That is, people are tied to only a few others, commonly by dyadic networks rather than united into larger groups. Kinship relations tend to be ego-centered, traced bilaterally, through both mother and father, and are limited in scope. The result is that kinship networks are restricted and large kinship groups are not formed. No basis exists for strong social solidarity among community members and resentments fester.

Nomads in the Middle East are commonly tribal, defined by anthropologists as being part of an independent, regional political grouping made up of structurally similar segments. In the Middle East, tribes and tribal segments are patrilineages, groupings of the male and female descendants through the male line of a common male ancestor. In practice, some tribes are tied closely to the state and to a degree dependent upon it; while at the other extreme, there are tribes entirely independent, and actively hostile to the state, and even entirely separate from the state-dominated society. Between these extremes, there are many degrees of independence and dependence. Furthermore, tribesmen might be integrated into state-controlled economic markets, while maintaining a high degree of political and military independence.

Each tribesman is part of a series of nested patrilineages, the smallest defined by close ancestors, and the larger defined by more-distant ancestors. Each lineage at every level has the responsibility to assist and defend each member. Lineages also collectively hold important economic resources, such as pasture and water. There is thus an institutionalized mutual dependence among all members. As a result, social solidarity and cohesion, *asabiyya*, is commonly found amongst tribesmen.

Let us return to our Yemen example, for it illustrates well not only the divide between the agricultural peasantry and the pastoral tribesmen, but also shows some of the characteristic relations between these groups. According to Bujra (1971: 5), "the Hadramis have traditionally seen their society as being composed of the 'civilized' people (*hadr*) of the towns and the 'primitive' tribesmen (*bedu*) . . . between the cultured townsmen living in tall houses, and the primitive, half-naked armed tribesmen roaming the plateaux and the valleys."

The contrast between *bedu* and *hadr* is mainly in terms of technological and organizational complexity. The towns represent large communities that are highly stratified and have a complex economy based on cultivation, trading, and a high degree of division of labour. They are also centres of religious and educational activities, hence the culture and sophistication of townspeople. By contrast, the small rural communities are made up of homogeneous agnatic [patrilineal] groups of tribesmen living in hamlets and tents. Their simple economy is based on cultivation, animal husbandry, and sometimes on caravan transportation. They depend on towns for their tools and imported goods and food. Schools and mosques, as symbols of formal educational institutions and corporate religious life, are not found in these communities. Hence the primitiveness and lack of sophistication of tribesmen. (Bujra 1971: 6)

The differences between the Yemeni *hadr* and *bedu* go well beyond ways of making a living and degree of sophistication. Their political organization is quite divergent. The towns are politically centralized, hierarchical, stratified, and peaceful; the tribes are decentralized, egalitarian, and warlike. Bujra (1971: 6) explains:

The large towns have always been under the rule of one of two Sultans. . . . They have always had centralized political systems and elaborate administrations. . . . [They were] religious sanctuaries . . . ultimately justified in terms of the supernatural power of their rulers. . . . All areas outside the towns, however, were tribal areas, in which each tribe had its own demarcated territory. Within the tribe, political organization followed the familiar lines of the segmentary system. Each tribe was divided into increasingly smaller segments down to the smallest unit which was generally a lineage living in a village or a hamlet. Within and between tribes there were endemic feuds at the root of which was competition for scarce resources and for the politically significant quality of 'honour.' Tribesmen, unlike townsmen, were armed with rifles and besides conducting feuds often engaged in highway robbery on caravans owned by townspeople.

Among the tribesmen themselves, there were "intense and widespread tribal feuds in the country," including the plateaus and the valleys (Bujra 1971: 7).

> The unarmed townsmen could not look after their farms which were always outside the perimeter of towns, and thus had to get protection from tribesmen. The Sultans were militarily weak and their territories limited to the large towns. They had treaties with tribes demarcating the boundaries of their towns from tribal areas. They even paid tribute in the form of gifts to some of the larger tribes, and when a Sultan wanted to move from one town to another in his territory, he had to pass through tribal territory with a heavily armed guard.

In spite of the dichotomy between *hadr* and *bedu*, there was continuous movement of people and goods between country and town. Internal and external trade was important to both groups, and it was in their interest to ensure that this was possible. There were three important social mechanisms that made this possible. First, there were various mechanisms in the tribal system that made possible the movement of people and goods. One was the "safe conduct" that allowed a person, with the aid of a third party, to cross enemy territory. Second, many of the towns were religious sanctuaries, *hawtah*. As such, the tribesmen granted them, commonly in written guarantees, a neutral status that allowed coming and going, and precluded conflict. Third, there were many religious figures in Hadrami society, including the reputed descendants of the Prophet, and those of past Hadrami saints and scholars. These individuals with sacred status served as mediators among the tribesmen and between tribesmen and townsmen (Bujra 1971: 8–9).

Social Relations and Production

Tribal organization—a regional grouping that ties together a large number of individuals and small groups in the Middle East, commonly in terms of notions of common descent through the male line—is important for pastoral production because it gives pastoral nomads access to a large region. Pastoralism, raising livestock on natural range, is an extensive form of production using a large expanse of area. Precipitation is sparse, and spatially and temporally variable, and in consequence, so is pasture and water. Livestock must range widely, grazing and browsing where they find grass and bushes, drinking where they find water. Middle Eastern pastoralists spend much of their time trying to ascertain where they should move their animals, and then packing up to migrate with them.

Tribal organization gives pastoralists access to a large expanse in several ways. Individuals and small lineages, as part of the tribe, have access to tribal resources and ties with other tribal members. There are two main aspects to this. First, the tribe often holds critical resources, such as land and pasture and water, in collective ownership, such that each and every member has a right to gain access. These rights are recognized by all and generally honored. Second, being part of a large group of kinsmen, individuals can generally find fairly close kin wherever they go in the tribal territory. This means that there is always warm welcome and hospitality. Nomads in search of pasture and water for their flocks and herds can therefore usually seek the aid of kinsmen in finding what they need and in gaining a comfortable and safe place to stay.

The importance of the tribal framework is well illustrated by the Sarhadi tribes of Iranian Baluchistan (Salzman 2000). Each of the tribes, numbering in the few thousands each, has a known and delimited territory. Every member of a tribe has full access to the entire territory, including a right to use all public resources, defined as resources provided by God and not developed by human labor, such as natural pasture and natural water sources. These public resources are freely available to all members of the tribe. Exempted from this access are resources made available by human labor, including wells, cultivated crops, and water control works, such as irrigation channels or flood retaining walls, all of which belong to those tribesmen who made and maintain them.

Sarhadi tribesmen can move without restriction around their tribal territory to exploit natural resources and to relocate their residence. This opportunity the tribesmen, who live in black, goat hair tents, take advantage of on a regular basis. Constantly searching for pasture and water for their goats, sheep, and camels, they migrate frequently to gain access to better resources for their animals. A dozen migrations a year are not unusual. Given the sparse and unreliable nature of precipitation and vegetation in this arid land, raising livestock is only possible by moving the animals around to where the pasture and water happen to appear at a particular moment. Tribesmen will also migrate to escape from human or animal disease, overcrowded conditions, and from threat or conflict. Outsiders, members of other tribes, must request permission of the tribe controlling the territory to enter and use the natural resources. Permission to use human constructions, such as wells, would require consent by those who built and maintained them.

What is evident from considering the resources held collectively by tribesmen is that the tribe is much more than the collected families of the members. Families are sometimes referred to, by social scientists, as the "basic units" of society, but this characterization is, in important ways, misleading. Families can pursue their activities and goals because they do so within a larger social framework that, in the case of tribal nomads, is defined by the constitution of the tribe. In the

Middle East, it is the tribe that provides access to many necessary material resources and guarantees security for its members. It is the tribal descent system that defines relationships among individuals and groups. Without the tribal framework, life would be a war of all against all.

INDIVIDUAL AND COLLECTIVITY

Notwithstanding the dependence of the individual and individual family upon the constitution and institutions of the broader collectivities, there is always a degree of tension and a certain discrepancy of interest between the individual and collectivity. Another way to put this is that there are discrepancies and tensions among various members of the collectivity, such that disagreements and conflicts arise over interpretations of rules and over decisions to be made.

These differences between people often show up in production and in the small local groups in which production takes place. Local groups among Middle Eastern nomads are commonly based on some combination of kinship ties and contractual agreement. In the Sarhadi tribes of Iranian Baluchistan, a small group of *wasildar*, or herd owners, usually based on a core group of patrilineal kinsmen, contracts with a shepherd to care for their flock for a year (Salzman 2000). This contract, *karar*, defines the local residence group, a mobile community of family tents. Annually these groups of tribesmen decide whom they want to hire to herd for them, and whom they want to include in the contract and thus live with for the next year, including or excluding individuals and families according to their judgments. Close kin are usually included; more-distant kin will be included or excluded according to how well they work with the others and how closely their priorities fit with those of the others.

Sarhadi tribesmen, and tribesmen pretty much everywhere, can, in their productive activities, differ from one another in their interests, talents, and inclinations. Some love their livestock and specialize their efforts in raising their animals, and are always ready to make heroic efforts to find their animals good pasture and water, no matter how far and how often they must migrate. Some tribesmen prefer to diversify, complementing their livestock with cultivation, either opportunistic based on rainfall runoff, or reliable but arduous cultivation based on irrigation and its tight watering schedule. These tribesmen, especially those engaged in irrigation cultivation, must work their fields regularly and cannot venture off too far. Yet other tribesmen are drawn to opportunities beyond the tribal boundaries, whether predatory raiding, as in the old times, or the more recent migrant labor and trading. These tribesmen must leave the territory and leave their affairs under the supervision of others.

When production decisions have to be made, for example, where and when to move the herds and thus for the community to migrate, different people's priorities diverge and their preferred strategies differ. Those specializing in livestock want to migrate more often and farther. Those engaging in cultivation want to stay within a reasonable range of access. Those who want to leave for work outside reduce the manpower available for migration, and throw responsibility on others. Even among the pastoral specialists, those with more camels look for areas with vegetation that camels favor, while those with sheep look for areas with vegetation congenial to sheep. So collective decisions are a process of discussion, argument, and compromise among the divergent interests and inclinations of the various individual constituents. Sometimes the process works reasonably smoothly; sometimes not.

In a Baluchi herding camp that I lived in off and on over years and knew fairly well, one of the enthusiastic herders was

Haji Reis, who tended to advocate an aggressive migration policy. One spring Haji Reis convinced his close kin in the camp, which consisted mainly of two mini-lineages of the Dadolzai lineage, to migrate to some far point in the tribal territory. The members of the other mini-lineage, who were engaged in a variety of productive activities, felt that this migration did not suit their interests. When the camp packed up to migrate, Haji Reis's mini-lineage headed off in one direction, but the members of the other mini-lineage headed off in a different direction, splitting the group. The members of the old group remained divided for a year, with some regret and some bitterness. When the two mini-lineages joined up again, it was with many warnings to Haji Reis to "back off," which he did, keeping for a time a low profile in discussions of camp decisions.

PEASANT DEPENDENCE AND TRIBAL INDEPENDENCE

What explains the different social and political situations of Middle Eastern peasant cultivators and tribal pastoralists? The difference in good part reflects the different ways that they make their livings. Peasants are sedentary, tied to their land, water, and crops, while tribesmen are nomadic, moving around difficult remote regions. Furthermore, peasants tend to be densely concentrated on the ground, in water-rich areas around rivers, irrigation systems, or on moist flanks; pastoral tribesmen, in contrast, are spread thinly across plains, deserts, and mountains.

From the point of view of states—which we should think of as cliques determined to impose their power on others for the pleasure of dominance and the profit of extortion—peasant cultivators are vulnerable and rewarding targets. Such cultivators are vulnerable because they cannot escape without sacrificing their means of making a living. They are rewarding because there is a high level of productivity in a small geographical area, which makes it relatively easy to monitor and control. Peasants, trained by their circumstances to proceed patiently through the seasons and the plant growth cycle, are generally not encouraged to be proactive or to develop initiative.

The townsmen irrigation cultivators of the Hadramaut in southern Yemen exemplify this clearly (Bujra 1971). These peasants live in towns that are either under the governance of a sultan or that are independent city-states governed by a holy lineage descended from the Prophet. These are mini-states, to be sure, but they are characterized, like larger, pre-industrial states, by hierarchical and centralized political control, and stratification of traditional status groups. The ruling group in the town of Hureidah, the Sadah descendants of the Prophet, made up 30 percent of the population and were able to maintain their position as the wealthy of the town. They were able to lead as heads of a moral community, and did not rely heavily upon coercion. But they could call upon allies among the tribesmen, whose ultimate sanction was violence.

A somewhat starker use of the threat of coercion was evident in southern Baluchistan (Salzman 1978). The *shahri* irrigation cultivators were ruled by small families of *hakom* rulers. The *hakomzat*, the ruling families, monopolized the water and the *shahri* peasants worked as sharecroppers for the *hakomzat*. As usual with peasantry, the *shahri* traced their relations bilaterally, and were divided into small, unrelated families. The *hakom* relied on the tent-dwelling nomads of the countryside, the *baluch* as their strong arms in case of trouble. The *baluch* nomads benefited through gifts of oasis products and by having a higher status than *shahri* peasants.

In comparison to peasant cultivators, pastoral nomads are a different thing altogether. First, they are much less vulnerable than cultivators to state importunity. Both the main capital resource, livestock, and household shelter and equipment are mobile. This means that it is easy for them to retreat and escape from any intrusion meant to gain control over them. As well, nomadism and pastoral production require constant decisions and proactive initiatives, instilling willfulness and independence. Furthermore, nomads famously live a hardy life in difficult natural conditions, and equally famously develop from childhood skills of riding and shooting that train them as tough irregular cavalry, for which they get occasional practice by predatory raiding. Both the tribesmen's mobility and guerilla prowess, as well as their spatial distribution, make them less vulnerable than peasants to effective state intrusion and control. This is of course all known well by state agents, and guides state strategies. And even in the unlikely event that the state could impose effective control over the nomads in their vast territories, there are serious spatial impediments to imposing and maintaining control over nomads who are spread thinly across the landscape with few in any particular area. The cost of policing and maintaining control would likely be much higher than what taxes could be extracted from the relatively small number of tribesmen.

The attitude of the Turkish Ottoman authorities of Libya during the first decades of the twentieth century reflects these attitudes (Evans-Pritchard 1949: ch. 5). Evans-Pritchard (1949: 90), himself sympathetic to the Bedouin tribes, appreciated the realism of the Turkish approach:

> The Turks well understood that the successful practice of the art of administration depends not only on attention to some things but no less on inattention to others. They did not confuse government with bureaucratic interference in the name of moral regeneration.

The Cyrenaican Bedouin had established close ties with the Sufi religious order, the Sanusiya, the headquarters of which was located in the south of Cyrenaica toward the Sahara. This was not a great concern of the Turks, who were used to religious orders in their empire:

> The local Turkish officials were content for the most part to sit in the towns [on the northern coast] . . . and to let the Sanusiya control the interior as long as taxes were paid and no overt act was committed against the Sultan's authority which might bring them to the notice of the Court; and the Central Government for its part was quite prepared to forget that Cyrenaica formed part of the Sultan's dominions so long as there was peace there and it sent annual tribute to Istanbul. . . . [Local Ottoman officials] therefore left the Sanusiya to perform many of the functions of government in the interior—education, justice, the maintenance of security, and even to some extent the collection of taxes. (Evans-Pritchard 1949: 92–93)

But the Sanusiya, although performing political and administrative functions, did not dominate the Bedouin (Evans-Pritchard 1949: 99). "Ultimately it was the tribes who called the tune to both the Turkish Government and the Sanusiya Order." The Turks did not have the large military force available to conquer the Bedouin, and the Order depended upon moral influence, which the tribal Shaikhs (Sheikhs) accepted in principle but not necessarily in practice. "Both Administration and Order were therefore compelled to compromise in their dealings with the tribes, who were, as Bedouin always are, at heart opposed to any interference and restriction."

State authorities do not, however, always take a modest compromising attitude in dealing with tribes. The Ottomans tended to be a bit more stringent in their own heartland. If tribes in Anatolia were deemed to be too independent, too rowdy, the government responded rigorously. Bates (1973: 33–34) reports on a Turkmen nomad tribe of south central Anatolia that was too unruly, and that the Ottomans forcibly settled. Reza Shah, the king of Iran, took an even more aggressive approach to the many tribes of Iran's hinterlands. In the 1920s and 1930s, he systematically sent his armies to attack and conquer the nomadic tribes—the Qashqai and Basseri of the southwest, the Lurs of the west, the Kurds of the northwest, the Turkmen of the northeast, and the Baluch of the southeast—and then forcibly settled them in villages (Arfa 1964). But this was not the end of the story, or the tribes, because when Reza Shah was deposed in the early 1940s, the tribes left their villages and returned to nomadism.

Most peasants are cultivators, and most pastoral nomads are tribesmen, because of factors already mentioned. However, there are some pastoralists who are under the control of the state and can rightly be considered peasants (Salzman 2004: ch. 5). Likewise, there are cultivators who live largely independent of the state, and who participate in tribal structures. Peasant pastoralists tend to migrate in regions with agricultural peasants and in the vicinity of urban areas. Tribal agricultural villagers tend to live far from urban areas and centers of state power; they are commonly found in remote mountain fastnesses, e.g., the Pakhtuns of Afghanistan (Ahmed 1980), the Kurds (Barth 1953), and the Berbers (Gellner and Micaud 1973; Hart 1976).

The nature of peasants and tribesmen can therefore be understood best in terms of their relationships with the state. Peasants are rural producers who have been captured by the state and are controlled by the state, particularly for the extraction of taxes and recruitment of soldiers. Peasants are socially fragmented because responsibility for collective action has been monopolized by the state, which forbids the organization of effective groups among the peasantry. Tribesmen are rural producers who live as part of a regionally organized, segmentary polity, which is to some degree independent of state political structures. They form into groups, patrilineages in the Middle

East, which have responsibility for collectively holding critical material resources, defending life and property through self-help, taking vengeance, and providing assistance and welfare.

How Middle Eastern peasants and tribesmen make their livings depends on characteristics of the Middle Eastern environment, such as,

- temperature and precipitation,
- ecology, as in the way natural resources are exploited,
- demography, such as population size and density, and
- technology, the knowledge of building irrigation systems, growing crops, breeding livestock, and designing mobile dwellings.

But equally how they make their livings, and how much they keep and how much they must give up of what they produce, depends on their relations with the state and its agents.

Intensive production in rich environments draws state control and extraction of taxes and services. Extensive production in remote, marginal environments can escape state control and draw lovers of independence. For this reason, how people pursue making a living depends partly on the amount and weight of state intrusion. If state oppression becomes too heavy, some peasants may give up everything and escape to the margins, taking up pastoralism if they can. Or if state control breaks down altogether, and peasant cultivators become subject to repeated raiding by nomads, the cultivators may abandon their villages and join the attackers, the only route to safety. Abner Cohen (1965: 7) describes this dynamic for Palestine under the Ottomans:

> This was a society existing on the fringe of the desert. When security prevailed, masses of bedouin tended to settle permanently on the land, in the valleys and the plains, living in vil-

lages. When conditions in the villages were bad—when taxation was heavy and the pressure of bedouin was strong—the villagers tended to become nomadic. Nomadism had many advantages. Nomads paid no taxes, were not conscripted into the army, were armed (while the peasants were prohibited from keeping arms), could amass wealth in the form of livestock without being haunted by unscrupulous tax collectors, and could even engage in occasional agriculture. They did not have to go far to the desert in order to be nomads, because large tracts of fertile lands in the valleys and on the plains were available.

Cohen (1965: 7, note 3) explains further:

> Nomadism in Palestine, therefore, should be seen, at least in part, as a method, or strategy, whereby the population protected itself against excessive conditions of insecurity and exploitation, and not mainly as adaptation to ecological factors.

Thus production is always influenced by ecology and economics, but also by political context. Understanding how people make a living in the Middle East requires that we consider political factors, such as pressure from state agents and from other population groups, as influences in the production choices made by Middle Easterners.

SECURITY FOR LIVELIHOOD

Middle Eastern peasants grew crops such as grain—especially winter wheat, barley, and millet—dates, vegetables, fruits, and nuts. Their main if not sole source of income was the products from their cultivation. The resulting stores of grain, dried dates, vegetables, fruits, and nuts were their guarantee of food and other necessities gained through sale or trade of their products.

For example, let us consider the property of the peasants of Hureidah in south Yemen. First, there are the capital goods, the property necessary for production: ". . . 590 acres, divided between 437 householders, gives an average of 1.34 acres to each. Each household has an average of 34 palm-trees planted on its land, leaving just under an acre to be planted with millet" (Bujra 1971: 58). Here the land, the water that irrigates it, and the palm trees, which produce for decades, are all capital goods, as are tools and livestock used to work the land.

Second, there are the products, the fruits of the labor: "In general the average holding of a household will produce 820 lb. of millet and 5,100 lb. of dates in a year" (Bujra 1971: 58). This amounts to 2.5 pounds of millet and 14 pounds of dates per day per family. If there are six persons in the family, each must be supported by around 6 ounces of millet and 2 pounds, 5 ounces of dates. If anything were in surplus, it would be the dates, some of which are probably traded for animal and dairy products, and for craft and manufactured products.

The loss of the millet and date stores of a family would leave them with nothing to eat or trade until the next harvest. Similarly, the appropriation of their land, water, and date palms would remove their means of production, and thus would make it impossible for them to produce new crops. They would be destitute and without prospect of survival on their own.

So too would Arab villagers of Palestine be (Cohen 1965), if they had lost their crops.

Until the end of the Mandatory Period [1948], the basis of livelihood for the villagers was subsistence agriculture. The main concern of the average peasant was to secure the *mūna*. Literally the word meant 'provisions' but in the living dialect it was almost synonymous with the word 'livelihood'. Securing the *mūna* meant the storing of the basic foodstuffs necessary for the subsistence of the family, and the family's livestock, for a period of thirteen months . . . a precaution against late harvest in the next season.

[Note 1] The main items were as follows: about 450 pounds of wheat for every member of the family, a smaller quantity of barley and millet, about 100 pounds of olive oil for every member, a quantity of onions, the seeds required for the next season's farming, and the necessary quantity of food for the livestock, mainly for the horse and oxen. (Cohen 1965: 19)

These villagers depended upon a daily allocation of 1.1 pounds of wheat and 4.2 ounces of olive oil per person for their *mūna*. Had this been lost, or the land, tools, and animals that produced it been lost, they would have been unable to support themselves.

No less is true among pastoralists. They depend for their livings on their breeding herd, which is their main capital asset. Aref Abu-Rabia (1994: 26) describes the herd of a Bedouin, Basem, whose home base is in the east Beersheba Plain. "Basem has a flock of 146 Awasi ewes, four rams, and fifty young lambs. He has a Peugeot pickup truck, two asses, three dogs, a cat, thirteen hens and two roosters. Basem owns no land." Abu-Rabia's study was carried out in the 1980s, when Negev pastoralism was market oriented rather than mainly subsistence oriented. At this time, Negev Bedouin would have to be considered pastoral peasants, for, although they maintained a tribal identity and affiliation, they had fallen under control of the Israeli state authorities and had to conform to the dictates imposed on them. For example, much of the land in the Negev was controlled by Israeli state agencies and could only be accessed by permit. As well, nomadic mobility was highly restricted and human and animal movement was closely supervised by state authorities. Nonetheless,

Basem shared with tribal and subsistence pastoralists his dependence on his herd for making a living.

Among the Basseri tribesmen of southern Iran (Barth 1961), each nuclear family needed around a hundred sheep and goats to maintain "a satisfactory style of life" by Basseri standards (Barth 1961: 16–17). The Basseri can be seen as a kind of middle class in Fars Province of Iran, in between the well-to-do land owners, on the one hand, and the landless agricultural laborers, on the other (Barth 1961: ch. 8). The Basseri can remain middle class and have a nice standard of living by local criteria only by virtue of their breeding herds, which produce expendable lambs, wool, milk, clarified butter, and skins, all of which can be consumed by the family or sold in the bazaars of Shiraz city and Fars Province. If the herd falls below sixty head, its products cannot sustain the family and there is a downward spiral as herd capital is consumed. Without a sustainable herd, the Basseri fall out of the middle class and must go to a village and take up work as landless agricultural laborers, with a corresponding fall in standard of living and prestige.

For peasant and tribal agriculturalists and pastoralists, their property is the base of the livelihood. Without it, they could not support themselves. The consequences of losing their property would in each and every case be dire. So it is no surprise that security of property as well as person is a high priority, and defense of property and person a major concern in social arrangements.

Chapter 3

FRIENDS AND ENEMIES

Security and Defense in the Middle East

The problem of security must be faced by every individual, community, and society. There is no more basic question than how people can protect themselves from attack, and how they can secure the safety of their persons and their property. In most societies, during most of history, property was closely tied to life, because property, such as land, crops, and livestock, was the source of daily subsistence, without which people could not survive.

STRATEGIES OF SECURITY

In the animal kingdom, strategies for security are genetic and hardwired. Among human beings, who rely largely on culture for specific behaviors, strategies for security must be established, institutionalized, and repeatedly learned from generation to generation.

Among strategies of security, there are two great branches: the branch of "self-help" and the branch of "authority." "Self-help" is a decentralized strategy in which all individuals take it upon themselves, either individually or collectively, to provide security by directly acting in defense and attack. All men, representing all families, are armed and ready to take coercive action. All men, excepting a few religious figures, regard themselves as warriors bound to fight, proud to fight, in defense of their families and groups. "Authority" is a centralized strategy for providing security in which specifically designated individuals and groups act on matters of security, defensively and offensively, on behalf of the entire population. Specific bodies of specialists—designated as police, army, judges, and prosecutors—are given responsibility for order and defense. They hold or monopolize special resources, including funds, weapons, and training, critical for coercive action. In contrast, the population in general is not supplied with these special resources, and is often forbidden access to them. The general populace is thus totally dependent upon the specialized agencies to maintain order and to defend them and their property.

In both branches security is based on established institutions; the difference between the branches is that for "self-help," all people and all parties are encompassed by and responsible to act through the institution, whereas for "authority," a small number of designated individuals are responsible to act on behalf of the entire population. There is a corresponding difference in recognition of social standing in the two branches: members of societies based on strategies of "self-help" are equal with one another and share the responsibility and prestige; members of societies based on strategies of "authority" are divided, with those in specialized agencies of control and defense having power and prestige, and the bulk of the population in a subservient position to those with power and authority.

Strategies of "self-help" thus lend themselves to more egalitarian societies; strategies of "authority" to more hierarchical societies. "Self-help" is characteristic of band and tribal societies; "authority" is characteristic of the state.

In band societies, with no more than a few dozens of individuals in each autonomous community, security from threats by individuals is left up to individuals, and security from threats by groups are taken up by the community as a whole. Among the !Kung San, also known as the Ju/'hoansi, of the Kalahari Desert in southern Africa (Lee 1979: Ch. 13; 1993), individuals will attack and kill others to block a threat. In this case and others like it, public opinion is generally taken into account in decisions to act.

In some peasant societies, subject to state authorities, but commonly distant geographically from them, individuals pursue self-help through institutions such as vendetta and an ideology of honor. In these socially fragmented peasant societies, whether agricultural or pastoral, individuals and individual nuclear families are the actors, as larger solidarity groups do not exist, discouraged by state authorities jealous of their monopoly of power. Individual peasant pastoralists, such as the shepherds of Barbagia in highland Sardinia (Pigliaru 1975; Salzman 1999: ch. 2) and the Sarakatsani shepherds of western Greece (Campbell 1964), use the threat of vendetta to discourage violation of the person, property, and honor, and, in the case of such violation, answer with the implementation of vendetta.

In tribal societies, politically autonomous or quasi-autonomous regional organizations, security is provided through collective self-help, with group membership entailing collective responsibility. Each individual is a member of a group with responsibility for defense, and must come to the aid of any other member of that group, and must take responsibility for acts of violence by members of his own group. Ibn Khaldun, 1332–1408 CE, who observed and took part in North African political life, described the tribal system and its relations with the state in detail. Ibn Khaldun (1967; see commentaries in Gellner 1981: ch. 1 and passim, Lindholm 2002: ch. 4) stressed the importance of social solidarity, unity, and mutual support among tribesmen, which is based on what he labels *asabiyya*, group feeling. It lies behind and is reinforced by blood feud. Group feeling and solidarity give tribesmen the capacity to withstand attack and to conquer. *Asabiyya* gives tribes the advantage over the premodern state, which is weakened by sedentary life, hierarchical stratification, and the suppression of aggression.

The segmentary, or egalitarian tribal political system was described vividly by Evans-Pritchard (1940) for the Nuer people of the southern Sudan. Evans-Pritchard showed that, without political officials or authority hierarchy, the Nuer managed order, security, and defense through groups that shared responsibility among their members for life and property. The Nuer could succeed because small groups faced off against other small groups, while large groups were opposed by other large groups. In other words, the tribal system worked because of balanced opposition. When men closely related conflicted, their small groups of kinsmen united around them. When men more distantly related conflicted, larger groups of those kinsmen closer to one or the other united to support them. Which groups were involved and which were activated depended upon how close or how far distant were the ancestors that divided the conflicting parties. For example, if there were a dispute between men with different ancestors five generations prior, their two five-generation lineages, *khamsa* (to use the Arabic term), would support them and face off against one another. But if one of the men from either of the five generation lineages were to come into conflict with someone who had different ancestors at the sixth generation level or higher, men from both of the five generation lineages would join together to support their member against the lineage of the other. And so on, up through tribal sections, tribes, and confederacies. The most basic principle was to side with the genealogically closer against the genealogically more distant. Furthermore, these kinship affiliations were tied to territorial ones, so that when members of neighboring groups conflicted, only those small groups were involved; but when people from distant territories conflicted, they were backed by everyone from each of their large territories.

In these segmentary tribes, each adult male took part in defensive and offensive military actions. Every man, a few religious specialists aside, was a warrior, in addition to being a pastoralist, cultivator, craftsman, and family man. All were obliged to act on behalf of the collectivities, from small to large, defined by descent through the male line of which they were part. They shared this responsibility, and were ready to act when the situation called them to action. Self-help was, for these segmentary tribesmen, an unquestioned necessity.

Choosing Self-Help or Authority

In anthropology, one conventional way to look at bands, tribes, and states is as an evolutionary sequence. But that is not my intention here. Rather, I want to consider the security modes of tribal self-help and state authority as they have existed and exist contemporaneously. Ever since there have been states, they have existed, if uneasily, along side of and along with tribes. It is only in the last centuries, and only in the presence of the modern, industrial state, that tribes have ceased to be a major form of organization. But where states remain more traditional than modern, and economies are characterized more by primary production than industry, tribes continue to have vitality and power. What accounts for the continued importance of tribes even in the presence of states?

While citizens of contemporary industrial democracies sometimes view the state with a certain ambivalence, on the whole, citizens tend to see the state as the source of security and benefits. But this modern, democratic state was very late coming. Premodern states, characteristic of earlier periods of history and widely present around the world today, are not democratic, and rarely provide security or benefits. The traditional state is more accurately understood as a center of power controlled by warlords, robber barons, and their coercive thugs, tax collectors, and priests, the latter supplying some kind of rationalization for the forced extraction from their subjects, who were seen mainly as livestock to be milked and sheared (Gellner 1988: 21–23, 103, 145–46, and passim). The main project of early states was predatory expansion, both for loot and for control over larger populations, the milking and shearing of which would bring greater returns. The peasant subjects of the premodern, despotic state were in an unattractive position, subject to abuse, extortion, and expropriation by rulers, tax collectors, and soldiers alike.

Tribal organization in many parts of the world can be at least partly understood as an alternative to peasant status within a preindustrial state. Independent tribesmen see peasants as oppressed, downtrodden, weak, lacking honor, and inferior. In contrast, tribesmen see themselves as independent of any interference, free to follow their own will, as equal to each other and to anyone else, as brave warriors, as honorable men. As a result, tribesmen actively resist conquest by states, resist incorporation into states, and resist domination by agents of states. To do this, tribesmen organize independently, on their own, in order to avoid falling under the power of the state. Tribesmen say that freedom is not paying taxes (Lindholm 2002: 25–26), so keeping independent of states gives them freedom. Given the choice, tribesmen choose autonomy, freedom, equality, strength, and honor, and avoid the weakness, oppression, inequality, and dishonor suffered by the peasant.

Tribesmen organize on their own to provide their own security through self-help. Groups are formed systematically based on an organizational principle, such as descent, and each of these groups is vested with collective responsibility for the security of its members. An injury, whether to body or to property, is regarded as an injury to each and every member. Here the moral principle is "all for one, and one for all." Each and every member is bound by honor to take vengeance upon the aggressor, who is deemed to be the hostile actor together with all members of his group. If there is a settlement, it is shared among group members. In a settlement, all members of the offending group are deemed bound to contribute to the indemnity. When an injury is outstanding between groups, the groups are known to be in a hostile relationship of feud, in which conflict could once again break out at any time.

Evans-Pritchard (1949: 55, 57) describes tribal formation among the Cyrenaican Bedouin:

> A tribe is conceived of as a huge family descended from a common ancestor, from whom the tribe generally takes its name. Hence its segments can be figured either as a series of political sections or as genealogical branches of a clan.
>
> A tribe is divided into several, generally two or three, primary divisions, or sub-tribes, . . . They believe that they are descended from a common ancestor, who is generally a son of the ancestor of the tribe. Primary tribal divisions split into secondary divisions, and secondary divisions into tertiary divisions, and so on. Each of the smaller divisions is a replica of the larger ones. . . . The members of each division also consider that they are descended from a common

ancestor who, in his turn, is descended from the ancestor of
the larger division of which they form a section.

Qabila is the word generally used to denote a tribe or primary tribal division. 'Ailat [singular: 'aila] are the lineages
into which a clan is divided and hence the sections of a tribe
of various sizes in which these lineages are found and after
which they take their names. Biyut [singular: bait] are small
lineages, or extended families, with a depth of five or six generations from the present day to their founders.

The political dimension of Cyrenaican tribes, like the
genealogical system on which they are based, is segmentary
(Evans-Pritchard 1949: 59):

> The tribal system, typical of segmentary structures every-
> where, is a system of balanced opposition between tribes
> and tribal sections from the largest to the smallest divisions.
> . . . Authority is distributed at every point in the tribal struc-
> ture. . . . [I]n such segmentary systems there is no state and
> no government.

Within tribal segments, of whatever depth and size, there is
solidarity and opposition to equivalent segments. "[T]hough
sections of a tribe may be opposed to one another they regard
themselves as an undivided group in opposition to neigh-
bouring tribes, and are so regarded by their neighbours"
(Evans-Pritchard 1949: 55). The operative principle in such
segmentary lineage systems is that, in any conflict, between
whatever tribes or tribal segments, people owe political solidarity and support to those closer in genealogy and are obliged
to oppose those who are more distant. This extends equally to
the smaller segments:

> The members of a bait have a lively sense of solidarity, and
> this is most evident in fighting and feuds. It is their common

duty to avenge a slain kinsman and they share the *diya*, indemnity, should they accept it in the place of a life. They are jointly responsible for a wrong any one of them may commit. (Evans-Pritchard 1949: 56)

Genealogy used as an idiom of social organization, as a way of thinking about human groups, and, although it purports to refer to biological facts, is, from the anthropologist's perspective, a cultural rather than a biological fact. This becomes obvious—even if it was not from the fact that patrilineal descent leaves out the female contribution—in the political sphere, when alliances of convenience parade under the genealogical flag:

> It will be found that in any of the main tribes stranger groups, sometimes of client origin, have attached themselves to the clan dominant in the tribal area and through some fiction, myth, or fraud, have grafted their branch of descent on to the genealogical tree of this clan. The Bedouin use the word *laf* to describe this process and they say that kinship established in this way may become as strong as kinship of blood. . . . [A] lineage . . . often is . . . conceived of politically as an agnatic group . . . together with stranger and [other] accretions which occupy its territory and make common cause with it in disputes with other tribes or segments of the same tribe. (Evans-Pritchard 1949: 56)

Tribal self-help thus requires each man to be a warrior, to be ready to put himself in harm's way to defend militarily his fellow group members, and to pay for the injuries his fellows commit, by acting as a proxy and thus a potential target, and by contributing to indemnities. In security based on self-help, the most efficient defense is deterrent based upon an image of cohesive group solidarity and successful bellicosity. Tribesmen wish to be respected and feared by other groups.

Nonetheless, tribesmen not infrequently find themselves in feuds and subject to military combat. This often results in loss of life, in injury, loss of property, and disruption of normal productive activities. Now while the latter might seem a small cost, for a subsistence economy in which productivity barely covers basic necessities for life, disruption of normal productive activities can lead to severe losses of foodstuffs, housing, equipment, and capital resources such as livestock.

In Cyrenaica, tribal feuds and wars were ongoing and a characteristic feature of Bedouin life (Evans-Pritchard 1949: 50). One of the main motives was control of territory and the pasture and water on it:

> [I]n 1800 the Harabi and Jibarna tribes, which are now in undisputed control of all Cyrenaica outside the towns, occupied only part of the country. . . . The wars by which they drove out their rivals were long and savagely fought and many incidents in them still form part of Bedouin tradition. . . . Besides the migration of whole tribes from Cyrenaica into Egypt there has taken place an exodus of many tribal sections and fragments, owing to intertribal fighting, until to-day there is not a Cyrenaican tribe, or even large section, which has not some of its members in Egypt, often whole lineages.

Evans-Pritchard (1949: 160) calls the Bedouin "hardy wanderers of the steppe, whose history was nothing more than a long record of tribal wars . . ." Tribal political organization operated offensively as well as defensively, aggressively as well as to constrain the aggression of others. This should not be a surprise in the light of the conquests that built the vast Arab Empire, conquests of which Bedouin tribes were the sharp point.

> In its general outline the history of the Arab conquest of Cyrenaica is well known. 'Amr ibn al-'As, during the Caliphate of 'Umar, conquered Syria and Egypt and in 643

overran Cyrenaica, then occupied by Berber tribes and under
the nominal rule of Byzantium. . . . Bedouin settlement on a
big scale and the complete Arabization of the indigenous
Berber population took place from 1050 or 1051 in the
famous Hilalian migration. . . . [T]he Bani Hilal [tribe] came
originally from Nadj [in Arabia]. . . . Arab historians have
compared their migration to that of locusts or wolves.
(Evans-Pritchard 1949: 48)

Tribal life and self-help, with constant threat of conflict and
loss, are less than utopian. But most tribesmen would, given
any choice, prefer to be free warriors than oppressed peasants.
They would prefer to put themselves at risk in equal combat
than offer themselves as subjects to the less-than-tender mer-
cies of thuggish, self-appointed rulers and their self-interested
minions. They would rather take their chances as brave and
independent men of honor, than take blows as cowering livestock of a cruel state.

Our map image of countries as large territories delineated
by clear boundaries grossly misrepresents reality through
much of history and in many parts of the world today. It is
more accurate to think of state entities as centers of power,
functioning a bit like magnets, which control areas close to
them, but which lose holding power as the distance increases.
Over time, for many reasons, state centers gain or lose power,
and increasingly bring under their control or lose control over
more peripheral areas. Between state centers there are marginal
regions, often quite large, not under the effective control of
states and thus areas of independent political groupings, commonly of a tribal nature. These independent regions usually
actively resist intrusion by state power. But the struggle is
always an ongoing one, with states sporadically but repeatedly
trying to expand their control, and tribesmen consistently
trying to gain or maintain independence.

The Turkmen of northeastern Iran illustrate this pattern very clearly (Irons 1975). In the fertile Gorgon Plain to the east of the Caspian Sea, ten Turkmen tribes occupied territories running north from the Gorgon River. Tribal sections toward the south cultivated, while those to the north herded (Irons 1975: ch. 2). But during the Persian Kajar Dynasty (late 1800s to 1925), Turkmen sections and tribes engaged in extorting "protection" money from the Persian villagers living to the south of the river (Irons 1975: 67–68), and in attacking Persian caravans and raiding more-distant Persian villages for goods and captives to sell in central Asian slave markets. This was only possible, of course, because the Persian crown was not able to impose effective control over the Turkmen (Irons 1975: 66–67).

How did the Turkmen maintain their independence from the Persian crown, which claimed suzerainty over them and their region? First, the Turkmen themselves comprised an army of irregular cavalry. As members of segmentary tribes and tribal sections vested with collective responsibility for defense and vengeance, each man was a fighter, and each boy was in training to be a fighter. Living an outdoor and hardy life, and honing their military skills in internal feuds among fellow Turkmen and in raids against guarded caravans and distant villages, the Turkmen made themselves into a formidable force. When challenged by the Persian army, they were not greatly daunted:

> Occasionally the Kajar government sent military expeditions into Yomut territory in an attempt to exercise a degree of control. Battles occasionally occurred between Persian military and the Turkmen, but they were seldom a serious threat to the Turkmen, and the Persian military was not greatly feared. (Irons 1975: 67)

Second, Turkmen nomadism allowed them to escape any concerted effort to suppress them. Although the Gorgon Plain was sufficiently rich to sustain sedentary life comfortably, and thus from an ecological point of view the Turkmen could perfectly well have lived in permanent villages, all Turkmen, cultivators and herders alike, lived in mobile dwellings, yurts, and regularly practiced nomadism, although for very short distances. By so doing, the Turkmen maintained their mobility and always had it available as a political strategy of escape (Irons 1975: 69–71). The association in the minds of the Turkmen of nomadism and freedom is shown in a conventional threat that Turkmen used to intimidate villagers: "I do not have a mill with willow trees. I have a horse and a whip. I will kill you and go."

It was not the Turkmen tribes alone that stood aloof from Persian crown control. The mountains and deserts surrounding the central plateau of Iran were filled with independent, raiding, warring, nomadic tribes: Baluchi tribes (Salzman 2000) to the southeast, the Qashqai (Beck 1986, 1991) and Arab (Barth 1961) confederacies in the south, the great Bakhtiari confederacy (Garthwaite 1983a, 1983b) in the west, along with lesser Lur tribes, and the Kurds in the northwest. These tribes were constant thorns in the side of the Persian state, and, worse, threats against the integrity of the state itself.

Nothing could be more familiar to the far west of the Arab Empire, the Maghreb of North Africa, than this dynamic dialectic between the centripetal state and the centrifugal tribes. Much of the anthropological literature of Morocco is taken up with this tension between state and tribes and the sociopolitical process it generated. Gellner (1981: 180) believes that the kind of society found there is

> an important and widely diffused *type* of society, one which
> for lack of a better name (and without prejudice) one could
> call the Muslim or the Ibn-Khaldunian type: the kind of

society in which a weak state co-exists with strong tribes, in which the tribes have what might be called a 'segmentary' structure, and in which the lack of political cohesion is accompanied by a striking degree of cultural continuity and economic integration. This kind of society is especially common within Islam. . . .

This type of society can be exemplified by Morocco, where there was

> . . . a weak, town-based, religiously charismatic dynasty, respected but not obeyed, and tribes which were remarkably cohesive and militarily effective, yet often devoid of any cen-tralised permanent leadership. . . . (Gellner 1981: 183)

The division and opposition within Moroccan society was conceptualized in local terms (Gellner 1981: 196; see also Gellner and Micaud 1973: *passim*; Geertz, Geertz, and Rosen 1979: 13):

> . . . [T]he country was divided into tax-paying and tax-resisting areas: into *blad makhzen* (land of government) and *blad siba* (land of dissidence). The latter fluctuated in size but covered something close to half the territory of the country. The loose and fluctuating division of the land into *makhzen* and *siba* was the central fact of Moroccan history. . . . Most mountainous and desert terrain, and most but not all Berber areas, were *siba*.

Geertz (1983: 135) describes it this way:

> Politically, eighteenth- and nineteenth-century Morocco consisted of a warrior monarchy centered in the Atlantic Plain, a cloud of at least sporadically submissive "tribes" set-tled in the fertile regions within its immediate reach, and a

thinner cloud of only very occasionally submissive ones scattered through the mountains, steppes, and oases that rim the country.

There was a particular spirit behind this distribution:

> Political life is a clash of personalities everywhere, and in even the most focused of states lesser figures resist the center; but in Morocco such struggle was looked upon not as something in conflict with the order of things, disruptive of form or subversive of virtue, but as its purest expression. Society was agonistic—a tournament of wills; so then was kingship and the symbolism exalting it. Progresses [royal trips around the country] were not always easy to tell from raids. . . . If Moroccan society has any chief guiding principle, it is probably that one genuinely possesses only what one has the ability to defend, whether it be land, water, women, trade partners, or personal authority: whatever magic a king had he had strenuously to project. (Geertz 1983: 135–36)

Even as Middle Eastern states have taken greater control of their entire claimed territories, right up to their borders, tribal peoples safeguard their security and advance their interests by crossing borders and thus changing jurisdictions. The Rwala Bedouin of northern Arabia (Lancaster 1997: 91) have learned well how to use this strategy:

> The Bedu are well aware that [modern] governments are stronger than they, politically, economically and militarily. Any government could crush the tribes in their territory at any time but they don't, because the tribe's cause could only too easily be taken up by an unfriendly neighbour with unpredictable results. However weak the practical nature of segmentary solidarity may be in fostering inter-tribal co-operation, it is sufficiently strong for it to be a distinct threat;

moreover many armies are made up largely of Bedu. The
Rwala play a large part in this game of bluff and counter-
bluff for they are very numerous and can cross borders freely
and legitimately. The inter-state squabbles, which are the
norm in the area at the moment, can be exploited by them
fairly easily. Thus the affront to the Sha'alan [shaikhs], which
affected the tribe as well, when their land was confiscated,
was countered by a retreat into Jordan, which was hardly on
speaking terms with Syria at the time. From there they waged
economic warfare on the Ba'athists in terms of smuggling.
This had certain economic effects, for the quantities of U.S.
cigarettes smuggled into Syria were so enormous. . . .

How did this strategy work practically, and why did the Rwala
Bedouin find it attractive? Lancaster (1997: 112) explains:

The family camped in north-east Jordan and started up
smuggling. Tribesmen who had lost their camels in the
drought flocked to them and the enterprise was a success.
The sheikhs saw smuggling not only as a means of making
large sums of money quickly but also, as previously mentioned, as a form of economic warfare against the Syrian government, which, they felt, had treated them unfairly. Quite
apart from this, the danger involved appealed to them and
they (and many others) regarded smuggling as a surrogate
for [traditional] raiding. It gave them the opportunity,
denied them for some thirty years, of displaying traditional
Bedu virtues of bravery and resourcefulness and it provided
the money necessary for their casual generosity. The initial
capital for this venture, i.e. for buying trucks, goods and
arms, came almost entirely from the women, who sold their
jewellery. Traditionally jewellery has always been a bank
account. . . . Bracelets, necklaces, medallions and head-
dresses, mostly of solid gold, were ruthlessly broken up and
sold, the proceeds being put at the disposal of husbands,
sons and brothers. As well as providing capital, it financed

the family until money started to come in. The Jordanian authorities, ideologically opposed to the Ba'ath, tactfully looked the other way and the Syrian authorities were in no wise prepared for a major policing action.

Tribesmen have usually been determined to take defensive actions against incursions by state agencies and agents. They have often succeeded, to one degree or another, in maintaining their independence.

However, the quest for power is not one directional. Tribesmen see with some lust the wealth of the state and its dependents, and consider ways that they could cash in. Several strategies have succeeded over the centuries. One is to produce and trade with the state and state markets. A second is to provide, for a price, "protection" for communities and for trade. A third is to engage in predatory raiding. And a fourth is to invade, conquer the state elite, and take over the state itself. Each of these strategies is popular, and some can work well in combination.

SELF-HELP AND AUTHORITY IN THE MIDDLE EAST

Both tribes and states have had strong presence in the Middle East since the beginning of recorded history and even before. The geography of the Middle East is generous in the vast deserts and majestic mountain chains that provide relatively secure homes to tribal peoples, and also offers several of the river valleys and moderately watered foothills conducive to states. The deserts of Arabia are the home of the great Bedouin tribes and the base from which they conquered the Levant and North Africa, settling in the Negev, Sinai, and northern Sahara. The southern Iranian desert is occupied by Baluchi tribes. The Taurus Mountains of Anatolia offer a place for Turkic and Kurdish tribes. The Atlas mountain chain of the Maghreb provides a home for the Berber tribes. The Zagros mountain chain in western Iran houses Kurdish, Iranian, and Turkish tribes. The fertile hills of Fars in southern Iran, the Tigris-Euphrates valley, and the Nile are famous seats of states and early civilizations.

As well, the Middle East, being in the middle, between Europe and Asia, between the Mediterranean and the Indian Ocean, between the north and the south, was a transit zone both for trade, which provided many opportunities, and for marauding armies, which provided many dangers. Considerable organization in the Middle East, for both tribes and states, took place around these transit routes. For tribes, trade provided a demand for animals and human labor for transport, and required protection. Trade required stopping points and trade centers for caravans, merchants, and craftsmen, which often also served as administrative centers for states and which provided much-needed income to support the states.

In the Middle East and North Africa, as in mainland Asia and early Europe, tribes thus were and are part of a complex social, cultural, political, and economic field that also includes states, peasants, and commercial traders. Tribes flourished because tribal life was regarded as more attractive than peasant life by many, because independence, freedom, equality, and honor were seen as tribal characteristics, while oppression, exploitation, servitude, and dishonor were seen to be the condition of peasants. Of course, tribesmen were prepared to trade their independence for positions as rulers, which they repeatedly did by conquering states and setting up their own dynasties.

How are Middle Eastern tribes able to hold their own in this complex social field? As indicated above, the answer lies in how Middle Eastern tribes constitute themselves. And the central element in tribal formation is the establishment of groups. Each tribe consists of small groups, which make up larger groups, which make up larger groups still, which together make up the

tribe. Each group at every level is invested with the same important responsibilities, particularly defense and vengeance. Each
group at every level operates as a corporate unit; that is, each and
every individual member is seen to represent that group and is
a legitimate representative of that group and a legitimate target
for any feuding enemy of the group. Each member of the group
is responsible for each and every other member and their acts;
as we have said, anthropologists call this arrangement "collective responsibility." When attacked, group members are obliged
to unite to defend themselves; when members sustain injury or
loss, group members should unite to gain compensation or
wreak vengeance. Anthropologists call this procedure "self-
help," because people act for themselves rather than depend
upon officials or agents of some other organization or institution, such as police, army, courts, and so on.

As has been described above for the Bedouin of Cyrenaica,
Middle Eastern tribal groups are formed in terms of patrilineal
descent, that is, descent through the male line. Tribal people
think of these groups as based on biological kinship; anthropologists consider that these groups are based on a cultural
idiom that selects certain arbitrary criteria for group formation. In principle, descendants of each ancestor in the male
line form a group, or lineage. More-recent ancestors are apical
ancestors of small groups, while more-distant ancestors thus
are the apical ancestors of larger groups. Middle Eastern tribes
are usually called by the name of their founding ancestor. Each
individual thus belongs to a series of nested groups, the
smaller ones defined by more recent ancestors, and the larger
ones by more-distant ancestors. In this way, members of different small groups may be members of the same intermediate
group, and members of different intermediate groups may be
members of the same tribal section, and members of the different tribal sections are members of the same tribe.

If each individual belongs to many lineages, small and

large, when does he act on behalf of one or another, and how does he know? Anthropologists call these lineages "contingent," in that they do not operate all of the time, but are called into action according to the circumstances. The circumstance that calls these groups into action is conflict. The principle of affiliation used is "always side with closer kin against more-distant kin." This is expressed in the famous Arab saying, "I against my brothers; my brothers and I against our cousins; my brothers and cousins and I against the world." By applying the principle of closeness vs. distance, a tribesman always knows with whom he must side, against whom, and when to be neutral. Loyalty and honor requires siding with the closer. When an individual or group is equidistant from the two conflicting parties, neutrality is the correct stance.

Which groups are called into action depends upon the individuals who face one another in conflict. If the individuals have a common ancestor not far in the distant past, and the ancestors that differentiate them are therefore recent, the groups activated will be small. For example, if the conflicting individuals have the same great grandfather, the small groups activated will be those defined by their grandfathers and which consist of the descendants of their grandfathers. However, if the conflicting individuals must go back eight generations to find their common ancestor, then they will be in different tribal sections, and the conflicting individuals will see themselves and others will see them as members of these large groups, which will be perceived as being arrayed against one another. This structuring of conflict so that small groups oppose other small groups, and large groups oppose other large groups, is sometimes called by anthropologists "complementary opposition"; I have referred to it as "balanced opposition." Balanced opposition is widespread among tribal peoples in the Middle East, and is thus a dominant form of political organization in the region.

BALANCED OPPOSITION IN IRANIAN BALUCHISTAN

To illustrate, I will report a series of events as I saw them in Iranian Baluchistan (Salzman 2000: ch. 10). Members of the Yarahmadzai tribe (the descendants of Yarahmad) of the highland Sarhad region had descended in the summer of 1972, as they did annually, for the summer date harvest season in the lowland Maskel drainage basin, leaving their tents and flocks back on the plateau under the supervision of shepherds. Each lineage had its own settlement, *bonend*, in the date groves, each settlement consisting of a scattering of mud-brick huts with roofing of palm trunks and palm fronds. I was residing with the Dadolzai *brasrend* minimal lineage (the descendants of Dadol), of the Soherabzai section of the Yarahmadzai tribe. The main business at hand was the date harvest, which would supply each family with a staple foodstuff for the entire year. The tribesmen viewed the months in the date groves as a summer holiday, a change from their regular scene and routine. But even in Mashkel, untoward events could take place.

Karim's Palm Trunks

Mahmud Karim was furious. It was August 25, 1972, at the Dadolzai lineage *bonend*, settlement, of the Gorani date groves, at the Mashkil drainage basin. Some palm trunks that Mahmud Karim had prepared—shortened, smoothed, and split—for the roof of his new *ban*, mud-brick dwelling, had been carried off by Nezar of the neighboring Kamil Hanzai *bonend*. It was true, he admitted, that the trunks were from palms near the Kamil Hanzai *bonend*, but, he was at pains to point out, they were from palms belonging to the *kom* of Mahmud Karim's son-in-law Isa, and not to the Kamil Hanzai.

What Mahmud Karim wanted to do was to mobilize his lineage mates and gather up a party of men to go with him and take back the trunks, and to fight for them if the Kamil Hanzai put up any resistance. A number of individuals from the *bonend* joined Mahmud Karim in this foray:

MEMBERS OF DADOLZAI "WAR PARTY," AUGUST 25, 1972

name	relation to Mahmud Karim	lineage affiliation
Shams A'din	brother of Mahmud Karim	Dadolzai *brasrend*
Abdulla	sister's son of Mahmud Karim	Dadolzai
Jon Mahmud	brother-in-law of Mahmud Karim	Dadolzai
Abas	MFBS of Mahmud Karim	Dadolzai
Sharif	son of Gemi, other microlineage	Dadolzai
Shahuk	son of Reis, other microlineage	Dadolzai
Ghulam Mahmud	son-in-law of Ja'far, other m-l	Dadolzai
Id Mahmud	son-in-law of Ja'far	Mirgolzai
Abdulla	son of Baluch	Dorahzai
Suliman		Gamshadzai
Majid		Gamshadzai

These men, mostly young, carried various light weapons: *lart*, a stick; *tabar*, an axe; *sang*, a stone; *karch*, a knife; brass knuckles; a wand of flexible wire rods with a lead ball on the end; but no firearms.

This confrontation was spoken of by Karim and the others in terms of lineages, the Dadolzai vs. the Kamil Hanzai. As they saw it, a man of one lineage had violated the property of a man from another lineage, and the offended man called upon his lineage mates to assist him. The two lineages were equivalent *brasrend*, both being Nur Mahmudzai, descended from a common ancestor, Nur Mahmud. Usually these lineages were thought of as close. Not only were they neighbors, but there were some prominent affinal alliances between them, not least with Ja'far, the headman, *mastair*, of the Dadolzai. Ja'far's mother was Kamil Hanzai, so they were his matrikin. But this did not stop Ja'far from supporting Mahmud Karim and allowing his two sons-in-law to accompany Karim. After all, in this context—as my Baluchi informants rhetorically put it—it is the father's side that counts; one takes women from anywhere.

Among the Dadolzai party going on the retrieval foray, eight were Dadolzai and four were not. The first four on the list were immediate kin of Mahmud Karim, members of the same microlineage, and the same informal but ongoing "work team," as well as lineage mates in the Dadolzai *brasrend*. The next three were coresidents and members of the Dadolzai *brasrend*, but members of other microlineage subdivisions of the Dadolzai. The final four were associated with the Dadolzai, one as son-in-law and coresident and the others as coresidents. Of these four, two were from the neighboring Gamshadzai tribe, one was from a lineage more distant than the two in conflict, and the other was from a lineage that was structurally equidistant. It is common everywhere for parties in balanced opposition to include both lineage members and other closely associated individuals.

Why was there this immediate movement to an armed band? Why was not someone sent to inquire, or to try and settle the matter first? In fact, the group was not really a "war party," for its purpose was not to fight. Rather, the group was gathered together to retrieve and transport the trunks, a task for which a dozen men were needed. They armed themselves and were prepared to fight in case the Kamil Hanzai had put up resistance. But the question remains: Why was the response the sending of an armed band?

Among the Dadolzai, the sentiments supporting this collective action by members of the Dadolzai and their allies were several: First, there was the desire for immediate action to redress a wrong. Property had been stolen and had to be retrieved. The palm trunks were needed. Second, people felt that they had to come to the aid of their lineage mates, in this case Mahmud Karim. He was in need of help and it was their obligation to provide it. Not only was it right to do so, but Karim had helped them in the past and would do so in the future. Third, there was fear that lack of action by the Dadolzai would reflect badly on their reputation. If they would not stand up for their rights, they would be regarded as weak, without character, without *topak*, solidarity. Fourth, if they were regarded as weak, then others would not be afraid of offending them. They would then be open to all kinds of infringements on their rights and property by others. Their willingness to fight to defend their interests had to be known, so that others would avoid trespassing on the Dadolzai. It was for this reason that the Dadolzai sent an armed party ready to fight, rather than an emissary to ask and request.

As it happened, Mahmud Karim and his group retrieved the trunks without incident and brought them back to the Dadolzai *bonend*. The trunks—two large trunk halves and two small—had been in a grove near but not within the Kamil Hanzai settlement proper, and the Kamil Hanzai did not come out to the location of the trunks. The group brought the two large trunk halves, needed for the roof, but left the two small ones, with Mahmud Karim's agreement. The group was not able to bring all of the trunk halves in one trip, and thought better of returning a second time. Mahmud Karim and the others appeared satisfied with the result.

But the situation remained ambiguous and could not be left as it was. It was necessary, now that the trunks had been retrieved, to inquire about the original act of misappropriation and to find out whether a state of hostility existed or did not exist. A neutral intermediary, *mardi monjine* (in Persian: *mianji*), a man without membership in either of the conflicting lineages, had to be sent to the Kamil Hanzai to clarify the situation. Had a Dadolzai gone, and the discussion turned nasty, he would have been at the mercy of the Kamil Hanzai. Gemi, son of Pir Dad, of the Mir Alizai *brasrend* was chosen. It was said that he was a member of neither party and so was not in danger. It was not Gemi's job to make peace, but only to inquire and then to report the current state of the relationship. Had the report been of hostility, the Dadolzai, according to some opinion, was prepared to go off the next morning in an armed group and fight it out with the Kamil Hanzai.

The report that Gemi brought back was one of reconciliation. Nezar said that he had made a mistake, that Musa— whom Mahmud Karim had paid to cut the two palm trunks lengthwise—had told him he could take the trunks, and that he had not realized that they belonged to Mahmud Karim. He furthermore offered to replace the two halves of the small trunk that were left behind. This news was received with pleasure by the Dadolzai, who felt that they had successfully protected their interests. The Dadolzai said that they regarded the matter as closed.

Ja'far, answering my inquiries, said that he, in response to Karim's entreaties, granted permission for the group to go to collect the trunks. He said that they would not have gone without his sanction. But he had instructed them not to go to the Kamil Hanzai settlement itself, as he was not looking for a fight. He told them that they should fight only if they were stopped by force from taking the trunks. Ja'far felt sure that Mahmud Karim was in the right, for he had a report from Musa, who said that Nezar had taken the trunks by force. Even if Musa had said that Nezar could have the trunks, they still had to be retrieved. Furthermore, Ja'far knew that Mustafa, the *mastair* of the Kamil Hanzai and his *maskom*, would not be enthusiastic about a fight with Ja'far, and so Ja'far felt pretty safe sending his party out.

In this case, Ja'far went on, the Dadolzai had had to stand together against the Kamil Hanzai, for the Dadolzai were *bras-rend*, and the Kamil Hanzai was, for Ja'far, only *maskom*. However, he elaborated, in other circumstances the Dadolzai would support the Kamil Hanzai. If, for example, the Kamil Hanzai were to be fighting with the Mogolzai or any other more-distant lineage, Ja'far and the Dadolzai would support the Kamil Hanzai and fight along with them.

The next morning, August 26, Mustafa, *mastair* of the Kamil Hanzai came to see Ja'far, to make sure that good relations had been reestablished. He promised that Musa would bring along another split palm trunk to replace the one left behind. Ja'far assured him that all was as it should be.

The Greedy Camel

One reason for the nonaggressive response of the Kamil Hanzai during the affair of the palm trunks was perhaps their immediate involvement in another, more serious conflict. Only two days before the affair of the palm trunks, on August 23, 1972, a fight had broken out between a member of the Kamil Hanzai and a member of the Rahmatzai tribal section. The cause of the conflict was a stray camel eating dates off of palms. When Mirad, the Rahmatzai owner of the camel, came in search of his camel, he found it tethered, in the possession Rashid, the Kamil Hanzai date palm owner. Mirad asked that his camel be released, and Rashid said that he would do so just as soon as the dates the camel had consumed were paid for. The men argued, exchanged unpleasantries, and finally exchanged blows. It was said that Mirad, the Rahmatzai, got the worst of it. He returned to his settlement at Raja, where most of the Rahmatzai in northern Mashkil resided.

When the Dadolzai spoke of this conflict, they identified the parties as Kamil Hanzai, on the one hand, and Rahmatzai, on the other. But these labels referred to nonequivalent groups and levels of organization. The Kamil Hanzai was a *brasrend* of the Nur Mahmudzai maximal lineage, which was part of the

Soherabzai tribal section. The Rahmatzai was another tribal section, structurally equivalent with the Soherabzai, although much smaller in population. So the Dadolzai were seeing the Rahmatzai from the outside, and thinking of the Rahmatzai as an undifferentiated collectivity. Furthermore, as all members of lineages were deemed collectively responsible for the acts of their members, any and every lineage member was open to retaliation for injuries caused by one or several lineage mates. Thus, from the point of view of the Kamil Hanzai, all Rahmatzai were seen as in a state of conflict with them and their Soherabzai allies, and each and any Kamil Hanzai and member of an allied lineage might be the target of attacks by Rahmatzai. For a Rahmatzai, all Soherabzai were potential attackers as well as legitimate objects of retaliation.

The next day, August 24, three prominent members of the Kamil Hanzai rode on a motorcycle to Rutuk, near Gorani, to check on their date palms there. The Rahmatzai who live at Rutuk, when they saw these Kamil Hanzai, formed a group and chased them away. This was followed, three days later, on August 27, by a violent encounter between a group of twelve Rahmatzai and six travelers—Abdul Karim and Shah Bik, both Kamil Hanzai, Mulla Mirza of the Ganguzai, Isa of the Hoseinzai, and two women—on their way back to Gorani from Gwalishtanab, Pakistan. According to the Kamil Hanzai, the young Shah Bik was beaten badly and the older men, including the respected Abdul Karim, and the women were pushed around. This incident, as reported and perhaps exaggerated, caused considerable agitation among the Kamil Hanzai and other members of the Soherabzai. They vigorously and repeatedly stated that it was quite wrong to act disrespectfully to distinguished elders. Furthermore, the Rahmatzai had gone beyond equal, negative reciprocity, which would have allowed roughing up the young man, by interfering with the elders and women. This was deemed an unjustified escalation.

Earlier, on the night of August 24, after the confrontation at Rutuk, the Kamil Hanzai and other lineages of the Soherabzai collected together and talked about going to Raja to fight the Rahmatzai. As it was late and dark, the tribesmen ultimately decided not to go that night. But after the violent incident on August 27, the Kamil Hanzai and their allies were determined to act. Furthermore, some travelers coming through gave them reason to believe that the Rahmatzai was prepared to meet them in battle.

The War Party

The next day, August 28, groups of Kamil Hanzai and their Soherabzai and other allies, accompanied by this ethnographer, set off across the desert for Patingaz, a clump of wild trees located between Gorani and Raja, in the expectation that the Rahmatzai would join them in battle. They came mostly on foot, carrying only their weapons. Some of the weapons, such as light sticks, appeared to be mainly symbolic; others, mainly clubs, axes, sickles, and brass knuckles, were more dangerous. There were no firearms visible, and no defensive accoutrements. There were young and adult men, but also youths and boys, and older men and a few quite old men. Along with thirty Kamil Hanzai, there were twenty Dadolzai, twenty-five Mirgolzai, seven Mehimzai, five Yar Mahmudzai, four Dorahzai, and twelve Mogolzai, for a total war party of just over one hundred fighters.

The tribesmen seemed quite willing to fight, but did not seem passionate. It was only the individuals who were most closely involved structurally in the original conflicts who appeared to have strong emotions about it. Nonetheless, said the allies, they were ready, they would fight! One had to support one's brothers. This was the Baluchi way. People collected behind their *pusht* (literally: backbone), their patrikinsmen, and fought with them, never mind affinal ties with the other group.

Now while the Kamil Hanzai were the principals in this conflict, all of the other lineages of the Soherabzai were implicated. They were all closer to the Kamil Hanzai and had to support them. Three days before, the Dadolzai were ready to do battle with the Kamil Hanzai, and now they had come as allies to fight alongside the Kamil Hanzai. The reason stated was they were *yeki*, one. Kamil Han and Dadol were brothers, and were Soherabzai. The Rahmatzai were not Soherabzai. Brothers join together to fight their common enemies. Some of the other lineages—such as the Mirgolzai—that joined the Kamil Hanzai were not as close as the Dadolzai, were not in fact Nur Mahmudzai but rather the descendents of Nur Mahmud's brothers; but they were all Soherabzai, standing together against the Rahmatzai.

The Soherabzai stood together, but the war party ended up standing around, for the Rahmatzai did not show up on that day. Along with some of the others, I—having found a post at the top of a sand dune, my camera at the ready—was both disappointed and relieved at the anticlimax. I was excited about seeing tribal conflict, and observing firsthand how it developed, and disappointed when no confrontation took place. I was relieved, because I was not enthusiastic about violence in general or about people, especially my friends, not to mention myself, getting hurt. But, really, I had already seen the most interesting part of the process: the lineage system at work, dividing people up into balanced segments and unifying them in opposition.

The Enemy Within

One of the coresidents of the Dadolzai was Isa Rasul (that is: Isa, son of Rasul) Rahmatzai, who was married to Malik Hartun, sister of Mahmud Karim and Shams A'din. He had been living in the Ja'fari Halk, the herding camp led by Ja'far, on the Sarhad and was living in the Dadolzai *bonend* at Gorani. That he was living there was known by the Kamil Hanzai and others, and threats had been directed his way. The Dadolzai stood behind their Rahmatzai *zamas*, son-in-law, saying that he was under their protection, and, as a consequence, or so was the understanding in the minds of the Dadolzai, there were no attacks on him.

On August 29, as had been planned for reasons unrelated to the conflict, Isa Rasul left Mashkil for Khash. In Khash, he met Sab Han, one of the *mastair* (headmen) of the Rahmatzai, who had come to gather up Rahmatzai to return to Mashkil so that they could support their fellow lineage mates. By August 31, he had succeeded in sending a dozen or so Rahmatzai to Mashkil. Sab Han recruited Isa Rasul to return to Mashkil and join the other Rahmatzai. He agreed and left the Dadolzai, switching his residence to his lineage mates. It was said among the Dadolzai that, if necessary, Isa Rasul would fight against his Dadolzai in-laws.

Although the Dadolzai stood up for Isa Rasul, "bracketing" him off from the Rahmatzai vs. Soherabzai conflict, and giving him their protection, this dispute colored the relationship between these affinal kin. The argument (discussed in Salzman 2000: ch. 9), which took place during early December 1972 between Isa Rasul and his brothers-in-law and the other Dadolzai, and the bad feelings that so quickly arose, must be understood in terms of the bitter atmosphere of the broader Rahmatzai vs. Soherabzai conflict. This was what explained the disdainful comments about the Rahmatzai by the Dadolzai. Such sentiments were to a great degree contingent on the contemporary dispute, for if this had been a long-term assessment, why had the Dadolzai accepted Isa Rasul as a *zamas* in the first place?

BALANCED OPPOSITION IN PERSPECTIVE

This form of tribal organization, balanced opposition, the structure of which is sometimes called a "segmentary lineage system" by anthropologists, is brilliant in a number of respects. First, this is a regional system of order that can encompass hundreds of thousands of individuals, on a totally decentralized, nonhierarchical, egalitarian, and democratic basis. No officials or centralized institutions are required. Thus the autonomy, freedom, equal status, and honor of each individual are enhanced. Second, balanced opposition minimizes the possibility that individuals will have to defend themselves against groups, that small groups will have to defend themselves against large ones, that numbers of attackers will overwhelm. In conflicts, groups tend to face others of the same genealogical level and same magnitude. The very structure of the system builds in a kind of demographic fairness.

The genius of the segmentary lineage system is in the deterrence against conflict provided by the combination of collective responsibility and balanced opposition. In considering opponents in a potential conflict, tribesmen recognize that they will be opposed by a group of the same genealogical and numerical order, and that the possibility exists that they will receive as good (or bad) as they give. There is at the same time deterrence within each group, as those less directly involved in the conflict, and those with a calmer disposition, and those with ties to the other group through their mothers or wives or children, knowing that they too will be fully involved once overt conflict has begun, preach restraint and argue against hotheaded adventurism.

In addition to the constraint arising from deterrence, there is another major and much revered mechanism of social control that militates in favor of peace and stability. This is the neutral mediator, structurally equidistant in kinship from the parties in conflict, and active in resolving the dispute and reinstituting cordial relations between the conflicting groups. The mediator always has an evocative symbolic idiom at his disposal, because the conflicting groups are always, at a higher level of genealogy, constituent parts of a larger lineage, and, thus, at that higher level, all of the conflicting parties are kinsmen. Mediators are commonly drawn from the most respected individuals in the community, often from high status groups, and for their troubles, if they are successful, gain the greatest prestige in the society.

Among the Rwala Bedouin of northern Arabia, life and above all political life "is based on the premises of equality, autonomy and the acquisition of reputation. Thus no man has power over another nor can his authority outstrip his reputation" (Lancaster 1997: 73). The main way reputation is built is through successful mediation between conflicting parties:

> Person reputation is the basis of political power as far as political power exists at all. In a system where every man is equally free to follow his own bent and where there is no mechanism for coercion, the only political power available is the ability to influence the decisions of others. This rests on four factors: good information, the ability to give good advice, a reputation for sound counsel and an audience to influence. All must be acquired.
>
> The ability to act as mediator in this way is developed [by the individual] over time. (Lancaster 1997: 73)

Rwala, indeed all Bedouin leadership, is primarily about either warfare or mediation of conflict and settlement of disputes.

> The Emir and the sheikhs are scarcely a particular case: they are the same case writ large. Any ordinary tribesman mediates within his own three- or five-generation 'ibn-amm' [lineage] or, if he is well known, between other 'ibn amms'. He can never mediate on a larger scale because his reputation

range is limited and because there are no larger groups to mediate between until the level of the tribe. This is the job of the sheikhly family as well as acting as mediators at 'ibn amm' level for themselves and others. . . . The Emir and the sheikhs are mediators on behalf of the tribe with other tribes or with national governments.

The Bedouin model of leadership is typical of segmentary, egalitarian tribes throughout the Middle East. Tribal chiefs depend for their authority on reputation, and act as war leaders, mediators among the tribesmen, and representatives of the tribe in treating with outside powers.

Returning to our Baluchi illustration, let us consider the intervention of the Yarahmadzai *sardar*, chief, Sardar Han Mahmud (Salzman 2000: ch. 10).

The Sardar's First Moves

When the Yarahmadzai sardar Haji Han Mahmud heard about this dispute, in the last days of August, he returned quickly to Mashkil, to his *ban* in the Mirgolzai *bonend*. He immediately spoke with representatives of the Kamil Hanzai. On September 1 he went to Rajah to the Rahmatzai. His goal was to bring about a peaceful settlement of this dispute. The discussion was reported to me by several Soherabzai sources.

> Sardar: The Rahmatzai and Kamil Hanzai are all brothers, should not be fighting, and should settle the matter peacefully. You, the Rahmatzai did not call upon me to settle the matter, which was wrong of you. But if you would give the Hamil Hanzai 5000 tuman and two girls for marriage without bridewealth payments, the matter would be settled. After all, you man-handled Abdul Karim, an old and important man of the Soherabzai, and this puts the balance of blame on you.

> Mahmud Selim, speaking for the Rahmatzai: No, we
> absolutely will not pay. We are one *kom* and the Soher-
> abzai are one *kom* and the two are equal. The Rahmatzai
> is prepared to fight but not to pay.

> Sardar: The Rahmatzai should then give 3000 tuman, and I
> will see that it is settled.

> Mahmud Selim: No, the Rahmatzai will not pay.

From this point my sources differed, one source close to the
Sardar saying that the Rahmatzai simply refused to pay. But
other sources reported the following.

> Mahmud Selim: The Rahmatzai will not pay. And further-
> more, you, Han Mahmud, no longer have our *kabul*, con-
> sent, as our leader. We repudiate you as our Sardar.

Perhaps because the sardar himself was Yar Mahmudzai Soherabzai himself, they felt that he was taking the Soherabzai side.
Certainly from the point of view of segmentary politics, the
sardar was not structurally neutral, being in descent quite close
to the Kamil Hanzai, Kamil Han and Yar Mahmud having been
brothers.

> Sardar: I have come to make peace, even though you did not
> send for me. If you do not wish to make a peaceful set-
> tlement, you cannot expect me to help you when you
> find yourselves in difficulty. I have the support of the
> *dolat*, the Government of Iran, and they will use their
> force as I say. If anything happens to any of the Rah-
> matzai, I will not do anything about it.

> Mahmud Selim: We Rahmatzai are Pakistani not Irani, and
> are thus safe from Iranian Government interference. As

far as the Sardar and the Soherabzai are concerned, the
Rahmatzai are a separate tribe.

Now I must confess that when I heard about the Rahmatzai
claiming to be a separate tribe, I felt rather uncomfortable and
slightly alarmed. Oh no, I thought, the Yarahmadzai tribe is
breaking up! But, of course, what the Rahmatzai were
expressing was the principle of segmentary opposition, and
this expression really should not have been a surprise to
anyone, not even the ethnographer still feeling his way around
tribal life.

The Sardar returned to the Kamil Hanzai *bonend* and
reported the results of his discussion. While he might not have
been surprised at what he heard, he was nevertheless very irritated with the Rahmatzai. He authorized punitive actions by
the Kamil Hanzai and other Soherabzai. On September 5, a
group of some forty Soherabzai from various lineages, led by
Mustafa, *mastair* of the Kamil Hanzai, and including Mahmud
Karim and some other Dadolzai, set off for Rahmatzai territory. Having arrived, they spoiled four shallow camel wells by
filling them with dirt and palm branches. Mustafa alone had a
rifle, of ancient vintage, but he brought it into play by shooting
at a distant Rahmatzai, who sped off on his camel. Mustafa
was later reported as saying that he did not wish to kill anyone
but the leaders of the Rahmatzai, Sahib Han and Mahmud
Salim. Whatever Mustafa's intent, there were no further con-
tacts with Rahmatzai on that excursion.

Fear was growing among the tribesmen. At Gorani, in the
Soherabzai settlements, there were frightening rumors. One
was that Rahmatzai with rifles were sneaking in at night to kill
some lone Soherabzai. This one lost some of its power when a
particular rifle carrier was identified as a Soherabzai.

Around eight o'clock on the evening on September 6, a
group of some ten Soherabzai from a mix of lineages set off for

Gazeh, with the goal of continuing to the household of Azat, a Rahmatzai, at Kalesagon, in order to beat him up. But the news had reached Azat, and he had left for Raja by foot after sundown prayer at six. When the Soherabzai party arrived, only Azat's wife and children were there, and they were very afraid. But the Soherabzai left without taking any action.

There was no further activity on the seventh or eighth, but the tribesmen anticipated that fighting would break out again and predicted that this time there would be shooting. It was reported by some that the sardar said that Mahmud Salim, Sahib Han, and Haji Abdul should be killed, and that he would take care of any problems that arose with the government. Other sources reported that the sardar had said that these men should be beaten, not that they should be killed, although he did say that if anyone died, he would intervene with the government to protect those responsible. In any case, the sardar gave his *dastur*, order, for action against these Rahmatzai leaders. The tribesmen said that anyone who killed under the sardar's orders and was taken by *dolat* would be released at the sardar's request. But in spite of all of this threatening talk, no one undertook an attack on the leaders of the Rahmatzai. Perhaps the intent was to let news of the *dastur* sink in among the Rahmatzai and to see whether the threats would bring any movement toward settlement.

Meanwhile, in Khash, during the first week in September, Soherabzai and Rahmatzai were going about their business and interacting peaceably, with no sign of conflict. This was explained by the fact that there were no Kamil Hanzai present. Other Soherabzai would fight with the Kamil Hanzai against the Rahmatzai, but the fight itself was between the Kamil Hanzai and the Rahmatzai, and other lineages of the Soherabzai would not fight without provocation. Had Kamil Hanzai and Rahmatzai met in Khash, I was told, they would have fought.

On September 10, officers of the gendarmerie from Jalq

and Saravan—in response to a request from the sardar or from Ars Mahmud, father of the injured Shah Bik, according to the source—arrived at Gorani. They stayed overnight and the next day drove to the nearest Pakistani police station at Gwalesh-tanap. The gendarmes were investigating the conflict, and asked the Pakistani police to do the same among the Rahmatzai. They intended to communicate the results of their investigation to the Pakistanis and then they and/or the Pakistani police could act on the conclusions to punish the offenders. But these inquiries did not seem to lead to any decisive action or bring about any resolution to the dispute.

At the end of October, after almost two months of cooling down, with perhaps some pressure by the police on both sides of the border, a party of Rahmatzai came to the Sardar wishing to settle the dispute. The Rahmatzai were represented by Mahmud Salim, his son Said Mahmud, Abdulla, and Azat Han; Sahib Han did not attend. The Kamil Hanzai were represented by Mustafa, and Abdul Karim and Ars Mahmud, the injured Shah Bik's father, were also there. The Rahmatzai agreed to the 5,000 tuman demanded by the sardar for the elderly notable Abdul Karim. The sardar was pleased with this offer, and said that the Rahmatzai would have to provide only 4,000 and that he would collect the other 1,000 from contributions by other lineages. However, Ars Mahmud demanded an additional 3,000 tuman for himself and his son, and was supported by Mustafa. The Rahmatzai refused to pay the additional 3,000 tuman, and the sardar supported them. After lengthy wrangling, the parties failed to agree. But now the sardar was satisfied with the Rahmatzai offer, and was annoyed at what he regarded as the excessive demands of the Kamil Hanzai. So the sardar took the position that he would no longer support the demands of the Kamil Hanzai.

While this meeting failed to bring about a formal peace, the attempts to settle by the Rahmatzai and the sardar's repudiation of the further demands of the Kamil Hanzai took the edge off of the dispute. Some prominent tribesmen, such as Ja'far of the Dadolzai, thought that the dispute was on the way to being settled, and that it would be settled before spring, when the Rahmatzai customarily brought their herds to Garonchin. However, if the dispute was not settled by *hamin*, the summer date harvest, and fighting broke out again at Mashkil, the Dadolzai would once again support the Kamil Hanzai. As a number of Dadolzai said, they are our brothers and we must support them. Perhaps the Kamil Hanzai were asking too much and being unreasonable, and perhaps they should have settled. But for the Dadolzai fault or blame did not bear on the question of support; they would support the Kamil Hanzai. But, on the whole, the Dadolzai felt that the dispute was over even if it was not formally settled. The sardar would pressure the Kamil Hanzai to settle, and would discourage further conflict.

Through the winter and spring the sardar continued to think about ways to bring about a final resolution of this dispute. He told me that he thought that Mustafa was not holding out for more money, but did not want to settle. He did not know why, but thought that Mustafa might *bakshist*, forgive, the debt and close the matter. But he, the sardar, would not ask the Nur Mahmudzai or Soherabzai to *bejara kon*, to contribute to the blood money, as he often did as part of a final settlement. Rather, he would pay the 1,000 tuman himself, not as a member of the Nur Mahmudzai or Soherabzai, but as sardar, or he would accept donations from the Huseinzai, the third tribal section. But he would not ask the Soherabzai relatives of the abused elder Abdul Karim to contribute. It was a great offense by the Rahmatzai to have abused a respected elder. In other cases, when young men were involved, yes, even fraternal lineages contributed to the blood money paid by distant lineages.

Reprise

Between 1973, when I left Baluchistan, and 1976, when I returned, the dispute between the Rahmatzai and the Kamil Hanzai and other Soherabzai continued to smoulder, breaking out in flames from time to time, increasing in intensity in summer 1975. Some people were referring to it as *jang*, war. The events were described to me by Soherabzai as follows:

Dissatisfied with what appeared to them as an outstanding blood debt, three members of the Kamil Hanzai conspired with Sol Mahmud, a Mirgolzai, to kidnap Haji Nur Bik, a Rahmatzai then residing at Garonchin. Sol Mahmud, not a Kamil Hanzai and thus not a primary in the dispute, went to Nur Bik's tent as a guest and ate with Nur Bik. He told Nur Bik that Juda Han, the famous Mirgolzai smuggler, had buried some goods, and that he, Sol Mahmud, knew where they were buried. He proposed, because he could not do this himself, that he and Nur Bik go together and dig up Juda's smuggled goods. Nur Bik found this offer too good to pass up, and went along with Sol Mahmud. But what waited hidden for him was not illicit wealth, but three Kamil Hanzai, intent on avenging the blood debt. When he arrived at the appointed spot, the Kamil Hanzai grabbed him, hit him twice with a stick, and hauled him off to the elder Abdul Karim, the injured Kamil Hanzai party. The captors of Nur Bik asked Abdul Karim what he wanted them to do with Nur Bik. Abdul Karim said that he wanted them to do nothing, and that he would *baksh* (forgive) his injury. Nur Bik was then released.

Another incident, unrelated specifically to the previous one, but infused with the atmosphere arising from the general conflict, involved Isa Rasul. While at the Dadolzai camp, he fought with Ghulam Rasul, son of Harun, Mah Malikzai, Soherabzai, over a fifty-rupee debt. Ja'far and others broke up the fight and Ghulam Rasul left. But later he returned, accompanied by Halil, son of Kasum, Dorahzai, and Nezar Mahmud Mogolzai. In spite of Dadolzai intervention, Halil managed to hit Isa Rasul on the wrist with a stick. Isa then, accompanied by Rahim Taj Mahmud and Mahmud Hassan Rahmatzai, went to the *pasgah*, the gendarmerie station, and made a complaint against Halil. Meanwhile, the sardar had heard about this incident and came to the *pasgah*, accompanied by other Soherabzai of the Yar Mahmudzai, Zabedzai, Dorahzai, and Dadolzai lineages. Under the sardar's direction, all of the tribesmen formed a *diwan* (in Persian: *divan*, royal court, tribunal of justice), a meeting for deliberation. This *diwan* quickly degenerated into charges and countercharges, then slaps, and then, much to the horror of the sardar, the Soherabzai all fell on the Rahmatzai and beat them badly. The sardar jumped in to stop this attack, cursing and even hitting the attackers, but could not stop the beating of the Rahmatzai.

Then, in response to the kidnapping of Haji Nur Bik on the sarhad, four Rahmatzai from Raja made a complaint to the police in the provincial capital of Quetta, Pakistan, that Islam, son of Nezar, Kamil Hanzai, was not a Pakistani but an Iranian, and had no right to be in Pakistan. This Islam Nezar customarily worked on both sides of the border; in fall, winter, and spring he traded, using Mirjaveh in Pakistan as a base, while in summer he grew grain on his irrigated land at Gazu on the Sarhad, and then to Gorani at Mashkel for dates. As a result of this complaint by the Rahmatzai, Islam Nezar was arrested and taken to the police station. But Islam had in fact seen to the formalities and had a Pakistani identity card, and so was released.

The news of this complaint and arrest was conveyed, by some members of the Rigi tribe who were in Quetta at the time, to Islam's father, Nezar, who was on the Sarhad. Nezar then made a complaint in Khash naming Gol Jon, a *mastair* of the Rahmatzai, and three others, saying that they had had his son jailed in Quetta. All of these men were called to the *dadgah*, court, in Khash and told to make peace there and then. But the encounter in court degenerated quickly, and some dozen Soherabzai and Rahmatzai began to fight—at the court!—as a result of which six men were arrested, the others having run away and escaped arrest. Nezar, it was said, sustained an injury with at least some evident blood, a diacritic for Sarhadi Baluch of serious harm.

In response to the fight at the *dadgah* of Khash, and to avenge the blood debt from Nezar's injury, six Soherabzai— four Kamil Hanzai, one Dadolzai, and one Yar Mahmudzai— sought out Lah Han, brother of Mahmud Selim, Rahmatzai *mastair* at Raja, who was working at Karvandar on the Sarhad. Lah Han was beaten up, and some of his blood was spilled.

The beating of Lah Han incensed the Rahmatzai, some of whom made up a war party of sixteen men—a truck with ten men, and three motorcycles with two men each—to find some Soherabzai and take revenge. Salu Han, returning north by motorcycle from Garonchin, had the misfortune to run into this war party. They chased him and he sought refuge in a house, where he armed himself with a knife. Salu Han and the war party threw rocks back and forth, until finally Salu Han was hit in the forehead and some blood was drawn. The women of the house yelled at the war party, the members of which finally left. They then went to Khash and announced with some exaggeration that they had killed Salu Han.

Not to be outdone, and to avenge the Rahmatzai outrages on Salu Han, the Soherabzai—mostly Kamal Hanzai and Dorahzai, but including some individuals from the Mirgolzai, Mah Malikzai, and two from the Dadolzai—formed an even larger war party of thirty men on ten motorcycles. Their target was a Rahmatzai *halk*. But when they arrived, they found that all of the men had fled and hidden, as it turned out, in Haji Abdulla's residence at Neelagu. Undeterred, the Soherabzai war party searched out a Rahmatzai *halk* in Garonchin, where they found three men, one hidden under a quilt, and beat two badly, drawing blood.

The Rahmatzai went to the Gendarmerie in Khash and made a complaint against the Soherabzai. The Reis of the pasgah brought a good-sized contingent of gendarmes to find the Kamil Hanzai at Burienbella, but when they arrived the men had already escaped to the hills. Id Mahmud told me that they were not afraid of the *dolat* or even of jail, but wanted to avoid having their heads shaved! Better to be criticized for vanity, I suppose, than for cowardice or fear.

The gendarmerie called in the sardar and told him that if he did not stop this fighting they were going to hold him personally responsible and he would see what trouble they would cause him. The sardar, for his part, was just as irritated with this dispute as the gendarmerie was. To try, once again, to resolve it peacefully, the sardar went to Burienbellah and announced a *diwan*. The *diwan* was held in Khash, with perhaps a hundred men. The sardar, I imagine, would have said the standard things: this behavior was shameful; these events were making a laughingstock of the tribe; the Yarahmadzai were all one, all brothers; were they not big enough to settle this matter? But this time the sardar went further; he said that he himself would not tolerate any further fighting, and that he himself would support the gendarmerie in suppressing the violence and punishing the culprits. To that end, he explained, he intended to arrange with the court that anyone fighting would be fined 5,000 tuman. And this he did. In the end, the sardar succeeded in bringing about a settlement. No money was exchanged. The Rahmatzai was acknowledged to be, at that point, the most injured, but they *baksh kort*, forgave the debt. The *jang* of the Rahmatzai vs. Soherabzai was settled.

United We Stand

The events of the Dadolzai vs. Kamil Hanzai and Rahmatzai vs. Soherabzai disputes were indicative of the part played by segmentary organization among the Sarhadi Baluch. The initial events in both cases were threats or apparent threats to the property of an individual: in the first case, the loss of valuable palm trunks; in the second case, the loss of dates eaten by a camel and a demand for compensation. In the first case, there was fear that an attempt to retrieve the palms would meet violent resistance. In the second case, the demands for immediate compensation prior to the release of the offending camel led to a violent fight. In both cases, many other individuals were quickly involved.

The reason that others were quickly and, as we have seen, often willingly involved, was the sense of collective responsibility among the tribesmen. For a tribesman, the presumption was that individuals were not isolated but members of groups, patrilineages, which they represented and which would support them morally, politically, and militarily. The Sarhadi view was that all lineage members were responsible for each lineage member, and that each lineage member was responsible for all of the others. There are two aspects to this collective responsibility.

One aspect is that lineage members were obliged to protect and assist every other lineage member. In practice, this meant that one had to come to the aid of lineage mates in difficulty, whether by violent threat by outsiders or economic need, illness, or social distress. There was a strong sense of generalized reciprocity among lineage mates, and an appreciation that for those who relied upon you at one moment, you would have to call upon in the future. In cases of blood debt, each lineage member was obliged to contribute to the financial compensation, sometimes substantial, in any settlement.

The other aspect is that each lineage member was deemed

by all outsiders to be responsible for the acts and actions of all other lineage members. In this sense, members of lineages were considered not as unique individuals but interchangeable equivalents. Thus retribution by outsiders for an injury could be directed at any lineage member. So, for this reason among others, individuals were far from indifferent about the acts of their lineage mates. Any individual might have been called upon to pay for what his or her lineage mates did. There was thus considerable social pressure within lineages to keep members from engaging in unjustified and foolish initiatives.

For Sarhadi tribesmen, the social order that allowed daily life to proceed without conflict, which provided security of the person and of property, and imposed social control of people's action, consisted primarily of the corporate lineage system. In the absence, illegitimacy, or ineffectuality of hierarchical power in tribal life, order and security rested upon the collective unity of the lineages and upon a balance of power among the lineage segments. Balanced opposition among lineages was the best guarantee of peace and security by ensuring that hostile appropriation of property or injury to the person would result in retribution and equivalent loss.

The rights and obligations of individuals as members of lineages were of course spelled out normatively, but were by no means solely normative. Mutual aid, generalized reciprocity, and solidarity among lineage mates were not only nice things to do. Tribesmen saw these also as in their interests, for they believed that their individual destinies were dependent upon the character of their particular lineage and how members of other lineages perceived it. Everyone wanted their lineages to be seen as solidary, brave, and tough, so that others would avoid any hostile actions. Thus any act by an outsider that could be perceived as deleterious to the interests of the lineage had to be responded to in a decisive fashion, lest others see the lineage as weak and its members as easy targets.

The tribesmen believed that each offense against its members not strongly answered would lead to other offenses, and these would lead to yet more. In tribal Baluchistan, the price of security is eternal vigilance.

Who We Are Depends On Who We Face

A balance of power may have maintained, in a rough way, the security of the tribesmen. But what maintained the balance of power? Here we address two technical problems: How can a balanced opposition be maintained as descent groups vary in size and population? How can balanced opposition be maintained in spite of the advantage that several groups would have in ganging up on one group?

The size of descent groups depended upon, among other things, accidents of health and fertility. What happened to balanced oppositions when some groups were large, with many people, and others were small, with only a few? This was a biological problem solved by social means. A variety of conceptual manipulations and social alliances were used to ensure that lineages were large enough to be viable and to play their parts in balanced opposition. In some segmentary systems, such as the Cyrenaican Bedouin (Evans-Pritchard 1949: 56, quoted above; Peters 1960), manipulation of the genealogy justified contemporary lineages of the appropriate size. In other societies, such as the northern Somali (Lewis 1961), explicit forms of alliance were used to build viable groups. Among the Sarhadi Baluch, there was also some conceptual manipulation, as with the incorporation of the Surizai as a section (Salzman 2000: 237), although there was also acceptance that some lines grew strong while others petered out. Among the Hoseinzai, the grandsons of Hosein, apical ancestors of three strong lineages, became more important structurally than Hosein's two sons. Another important measure, which could be used to incorporate weak lines into unified lineages, and thus maintain viable lineages and a balance among lineages, was affinal alliance. Among the Dadolzai, the multiple intermarriages of the Shadi Hanzai and Dust Mahmudzai led them to act politically in a unified fashion vis-à-vis the other Dadolzai sublineages (Salzman 2000: ch. 9).

Even if all of the "on the ground" *brasrend* (minimal lineages) were a viable size, from 50 to 150 persons, what was to keep two or three *brasrend* from ganging up on one, if this were to be politically expedient? This social problem was solved by biological—at least conceptually biological—means. In the segmentary lineage system, contingent political affiliation was predetermined by genealogical closeness or distance, which was normatively privileged as the basis of alliance. One was obliged to side with a brother against a cousin, with brothers and cousins against more-distant kin, with other *brasrend* of one's maximal segment against another maximal segment, with other maximal segments of one's tribal section against another tribal section, and so on. Similarly, in a dispute between cousins, ego was structurally neutral and so was not supposed to take sides, although one could and perhaps should intervene as a neutral peacemaker to try to settle the dispute.

The genius of the segmentary lineage system is that, through this complementary opposition, a balance of power is maintained. The splitting or clumping of lineages according to the descent of the individuals in conflict ensures at least a rough equivalence of number among disputants, a critical parameter in a tribal setting where most adult males are potentially warriors. Through this equivalence, a balance of power is maintained, and through the balance of power, a degree of peace and security.

What I have called "balanced opposition" as part of a "segmentary model" was the way that Sarhadi tribesmen themselves looked at political alliances and action. This set of rules about alliance and political support was believed and asserted by the Sarhadi tribesmen. The disputes of the Dadolzai vs. the Kamil Hanzai and the Rahmatzai vs. the Soherabzai were two examples of the way that this model was played out in practice. In these disputes, the Dadolzai opposed the Kamil Hanzai and were ready to resort to violence, and then, as members of the Soherabzai tribal section, closed ranks with the Kamil Hanzai to support them in opposition to the Rahmatzai tribal section. While the principals in the dispute and particularly those injured were primary points of reference, and the *brasrend* of the injured parties, in this case the Kamil Hanzai among the Soherabzai, had the responsibility for taking vengeance, seeking redress, or accepting a settlement, other lineages of the tribal sections were expected to provide support and did participate actively in the conflict.

The position of Isa Rasul, a Rahmatzai married to and living among the Soherabzai, illustrated the power of lineage and sectional affiliation. Although under the protection of his affines, i.e., in-laws through marriage, the Dadolzai, Isa remained under threat from other Soherabzai. But more important was his obligation to come to the aid of his patrikin, even to the extent of having to fight his own affines. It was this obligation that led him to change residence, leaving his affines and returning to the Rahmatzai. The ongoing dispute between his Rahmatzai lineage mates and his Soherabzai affines soured relations between him and his affines, which resulted in an angry dispute between Isa and the Dadolzai.

In the general dispute between the tribal sections, the Yarahmadzai sardar played the role of mediator. While his attempts were not very well received, he continued to provide moral pressure for settlement and ultimately for unity and peace. We can see that, in a structural sense, mediation is the lubrication of the segmentary lineage system, smoothing the transition from balanced opposition to reinstituted unity.

Tribal leaders such as the Rwala Emir and sheikhs and the Yarahmadzai sardar are not the only kinds of mediators in Middle Eastern political environments.

Some Berber tribes (Gellner 1969) have sections of religious specialists who do not carry arms or take part in conflict, and who by virtue of their pacifism are regarded as neutral, and who live by providing religious services and mediation. (Neutral religious specialists also play the role of mediators among the Nuer of the southern Sudan [Evans-Pritchard 1940].) We have seen that in Yemen, town leaders with religious status provided mediation backed by religious prestige (Bujra 1971). Among the Bedouin of Cyrenaica, *marabtin*, marabouts from the Maghreb settled and provided religious services and mediation among the tribes. *Marabat*, or marabout, tombs became shrines and cult centers for the tribesmen. These shrines were regarded by tribesmen as neutral and safe sites. It is notable that the shrines tended to be located on boundaries between tribal sections or tribes, in the same way that neutral mediators stood structurally between the tribal sections (Evans-Pritchard 1949: 66–68). Later, when the Sanusi sufi order was established in Cyrenaica, it took up this role of the marabouts. To do this, Sanusi lodges were built on tribal borders. "The distributions of lodges may be said to have reflected tribal segmentation, mirroring lines of cleavage between tribes and between tribal sections" (Evans-Pritchard 1949: 71–72). A neutral presence and mediation were major contributions (Evans-Pritchard 1949: 71, 80):

> The social functions carried out by the Sanusiya lodges. . . . Propaganda of the faith, educational work, cultivation of gardens, settlement of disputes, provision of shelter, hospitality, and security to travellers, and of refuge for the pursued, the weak, and the oppressed are all functions especially appropriate to tribal and barbarous conditions of life.

Livestock market, primarily for expendable male or aged animals. Zahedan, Baluchistan, Iran. 1972. *(All photos courtesy of the author.)*

Irrigated garden of palms and other crops in Saravan, south of the highland Sarhad region of the Yarahmadzai tribe. Baluchistan, Iran. 1972.

Migration of a camping group of the Dadolzai lineage, as they move to another camping location for superior grazing, better access to water, and avoidance of crowding and disease. Baluchistan, Iran. Spring 1973.

Used clothing market, where legally imported and smuggled goods, primarily from Pakistan, but often originating in Europe or elsewhere, were sold. Zahedan, Baluchistan, Iran. 1972.

Migration of a camping group of the Dadolzai lineage, as they move to another camping location for superior grazing, better access to water, and avoidance of crowding and disease. Baluchistan, Iran. Spring 1973.

Yarahmadzi tribal herding camp: black tents woven from goat-hair yarn with side panels woven from wild palm frond leaves, surrounded by brush for wood cooking fires and haze from cooking fire smoke, with a camel waiting at owner's tent for meal of plant roots. Photo taken from in front of author's tent in the Dadolzai camp, Baluchistan, Iran. Winter 1972.

A war party illustrating lineage solidarity in oppositional conflict. Members of the large Soherabzai section of the Yarahmadzai tribe united and awaiting the arrival of their opponents, the Huseinzai section, to engage in combat following a series of conflicts and injuries between members of these lineages. Mashkeel, Baluchistan, Iran. Summer 1973.

Ja'far, esteemed headman of Dadolzai herding camp, Yarahmadzai tribe. A pleasant, capable, kind, and gracious man, who was a fine and effective mediator and leader of his camping group, and a generous and indulgent host to the author and his family. Baluchistan, Iran. Winter 1972.

Shah Abbas Hotel, previously a caravanserai that served merchants and their transport caravans, with dome of Shah's Mosque in background. Isfahan, Iran. 1973.

The *Masjed-i Shah*, the Shah's Mosque, for which construction was started in 1611 by the Safavid dynasty in their capital of Isfahan, Iran. The *Masjed-i Shah* is one of the acknowledged glories of Persian architecture. 1973.

Mulla Rustam, Dadolzai lineage *mulla* (religous leader), trained in a Sunni Pakistani madrasse (Islamic religious school), who led prayers, gave sermons, and provided religious remedies for illness. Yarahmadzai tribe, Baluchistan, Iran. Winter 1972.

Tribal Chief and Provincial Governor meet. Sardar Han Mahmud, Yarahmadzai tribe (at left in turban) lobbies the Governor-General of the Province of Sistan and Baluchistan (right center, in tweed jacket and western-style hat) for various benefits, such as a diesel engine driven irrigation pump. 1972.

Inside a tent: Yarahmadzai tribal elder smoking water pipe (on left), young man with radio bought with proceeds from migrant labor in Abu Zhabi on the Arabian side of the Gulf (on right), woman (in back) spinning wool. Baluchistan, Iran. 1972.

> Each lodge had its Shaikh. . . . He arbitrated between the
> Bedouin, led the tribesmen to holy war, acted as intermediary
> between the tribe or section and the Turkish administration . . .

Whether tribal leader or religious figure, the mediator provided a complement to the balanced opposition of tribal segments, easing the way to settlement of disputes and peace once
the deterrent power of opposition itself failed.

How Pervasive Is Balanced Opposition?

There can be no doubt about the centrality of balanced opposition and tribal organization in the historical Middle East
from the rise of Muhammad and the rapid expansion of the
Arab Empire. Muhammad's Arabia was a tribal region, and his
constituency was Bedouin tribes who served as the shock
troops and colonialists in the Arab invasions of the Levant and
North Africa in the west, and Iran, India, and central Asia in
the east. Even such major religious splits as that between Shi'a
and Sunni were born in balanced opposition between two
closely related lineages in Mecca.

The Arab Empire and the Middle East of course grew beyond
their tribal origins, adopting and founding cities, and exploiting
the large, indigenous, Christian and Jewish peasant populations.
Islam, according to some scholars, evolved into an urban religion. This raises the question of whether, with these developments, balanced opposition lost its predominance in Middle
Eastern sociopolitical organization. To what degree has balanced opposition remained a major principle of Middle Eastern
organization? Let us explore some relevant considerations.

First, in the Arab world, the time of Muhammad and the
period that followed is widely regarded as the "Golden Age" of
the Middle East when Islam was pure, men were men, and

Arabs rightly ruled the world. Many Arabs look back to this age as a model to emulate and a goal to strive for. Tribal life is conceived of as proper and pure. The desert is the destination for purifying and revivifying. Tribal life is seen as the origin and the ideal. As such, even for those living in village or urban conditions, and making a living in sedentary activities, the desert and its tribal life is a constant, positive referent.

Second, there are today major areas of the Middle East in which tribal peoples make up the dominant population: In the mountains of the Maghreb, the southern deserts of Libya, and the western and eastern deserts of Egypt, throughout the deserts of the Levant and Arabia, the southern deserts and northern mountains of Iraq, and the mountains and deserts of Iran. In these regions, tribes, now mostly "encapsulated" by national governments, and thus rarely more than semi-independent, remain the main framework of organization.

Third, throughout the Middle East, many peasants have a tribal origin, some shift between village and tent life, and it is not uncommon for peasants to maintain group organization based on patrilineal descent. Tribal organization reaches beyond the nomads of the deserts and mountains to the peasantry and even into the towns and cities. Settled tribesmen bring their descent groups and feuds into their settlements, as we shall see in detail in the next chapter. And tribal notables, shaikhs, often take prominent part in regional and national elites.

The basic principles of balanced opposition continue to be operative in Middle Eastern towns and cities. To cite just one case, conflict in contemporary Gaza leads to blood feuds between kin groups (*Globe and Mail* 2006):

"They never saw each other as an enemy . . . Their families were always very close until recently."—Nasser Khalil, an acquaintance of two Palestinian friends in Gaza, who attended the same school, prayed at the same mosque and played soccer together—yet unwittingly found themselves on opposite ends of a bloody gunfight between two rival factions last week that claimed both their lives. At first, the families of both victims, Mohammed Harazin and Ismail Abu Hair, planned revenge against each other, as is tradition when members of one clan kill another. But fighters from Islamic Jihad intervened, fearing that the violence would spiral out of control. Finally, the patriarchs of each family agreed to respect a truce, which they tearfully announced in a shared statement at a Dec. 21 [2006] press conference: "From here this moment we declare our wish for this conflict to end. We are willing to forgive and forget the blood of our sons . . . We need to stop the blood flowing from our people."

In Gaza City (*Ottawa Citizen* 2006: A12),

Violent clashes broke out early today between Hamas fighters and armed members of a powerful family clan in Gaza City, with at least one person killed and one wounded, witnesses said.

. . . Fighting took place in the district where one of Hamas' top officials in Gaza, Foreign Minister Mahmud Zahar, lives. His home was targeted by the powerful family, two of whose members were killed Wednesday in clashes with Hamas, and the witnesses said several Hamas members were abducted.

Balanced opposition between kin groups is manifested in Middle Eastern towns and cities, particularly where hierarchical control is weak. Currently similar processes are dominant in Baghdad and Beirut.

Fourth, Islam firmly maintains the opposition between the Muslim and the infidel. As we shall see, the Muslim is opposed to the infidel, and the *dar al-Islam*, the land of Islam and peace, to the *dar al-harb*, the land of the infidels and conflict. Balanced opposition was raised to a higher and more inclusive structural level, and the newly Muslim tribes were unified in the face of the infidel enemy. We can see this manifested among the Bedouin of Cyrenaica, who, while they did not fulfill various ritual obligations with great assiduity, excused themselves by explaining "their enthusiasm for the *jihad*, holy war against unbelievers." The Bedouin admitted that they do not pray regularly, but "'*nasum wa najhad*' 'we fast and we wage holy war'" (Evans-Pritchard 1949: 63). With Muhammad's Islamic revolution, balanced opposition came to encompass the world, and to have the authorization of God.

Chapter 4

DEFENSE AND OFFENSE
Honor and Rank in the Middle East

Social institutions work only if people can be motivated to follow the rules that make up the institution. Middle Eastern tribal institutions, such as collective responsibility among kinsmen in descent groups, work only if kinsmen are motivated to contribute their scarce resources when blood money must be paid, to share blood money among kinsmen when it comes to them, to stand up and put themselves in danger's way to defend their fellows, to risk themselves in attacking the opposition when required by a lineage mate's loss or injury, and to proceed with their activities knowing that they are legitimate targets for the aggressive deeds of their fellow kinsmen. How are Middle Easterners motivated to participate in such institutions?

In considering motivation, it is useful to consider three types:

- First, there is *intrinsic* motivation, which is a result of innate pleasure to engage in the specified activities. For example, other constraints aside, most people will be motivated by pleasurable sensations to breathe, eat, defecate, and engage in sexual relations.
- Second, there is *internalized* motivation, which is brought about by our internalizing norms, rules, and ideals. Here we find the sense of duty, and a sense of guilt for not fulfilling internalized expectations. For example, we may have been (successfully) taught to share with the less needy, and if we do, we feel righteous, and if we do not, we feel guilty.
- Third, there is *extrinsic* motivation, the rewards and punishments that come from fulfilling expectations or not fulfilling expectations. For example, if we study and succeed on an exam, we are rewarded with a good grade; whereas if we do badly on an exam, we receive a poor grade. Similarly, if we work hard at our job and succeed at its specified tasks, we receive our wages or salary, and perhaps eventually a promotion; if we slack in our work, or fail in its tasks, we shall certainly not be rewarded and probably will be transferred to some less desirable job or fired.

How then do these types of motivations induce Middle Easterners to support their groups?

- First, in regard to intrinsic motivation, the release of anger in combat on behalf of one's family, clan, or tribe can be highly gratifying, particularly if expression of anger is typically repressed in daily life, in a social environment of strict control (Spiro 1973). In the Middle East, extreme respect and deference to senior kinsmen is expected of juniors, and this must be manifested in strict obedience. Discontent and anger must be repressed by the individual.

But such anger does not go away; it is stored and builds. In any aggressive action against legitimate targets, built-up anger and fury can transferred to the legitimate targets, and be released, resulting in the pleasure of release. Warriors, and these are commonly young men, can experience an emotional "high" in combat, transforming the internalized "duty" to fight into intrinsic pleasure. Once experienced, this "high" can motivate men to experience it again and thus to fight again.

- Second, in regard to internalized motivation, in ordinary "socialization" or "enculturation" of children, the ideals, norms, and rules of life are taught, and "good" is distinguished from "bad." A child's duty to his father and mother, his brothers and sisters, his kin group, his broader kin relations, his tribe, and his faith, as well as his righteous opposition to other kin groups, tribal sections, tribes, and faiths are enunciated, defined, explained, and driven home repeatedly and relentlessly. Middle Eastern children learn early their duty to obey their elders and support their kinsmen, and that only bad people misbehave and avoid their duty. They also learn early that righteousness demands vigorous opposition to the "other": the other family, the other lineage-descent group, the other tribal section, the other tribe, the other confederacy, the other sect, the other faith. The question of whether "my group" is right or wrong never comes up, because there are no external criteria that one is meant to judge it by. Rather, "my group" is always right, because it is my group always. These norms, internalized into the hearts of Middle Easterners, guide them to do their duty, and to feel the gratification of being righteous, while avoidance of duty results in painful guilt.
- Third, as regards extrinsic motivation, Middle Easterners can see the rewards offered by their institutions, and the

penalties for deviating from the expected norms. At a practical level, Middle Easterners see that their kin are the only people they can count on for support. For protection they must stick with their kin, lest they become totally vulnerable targets for any aggressor. Here, then, is enlightened self-interest: one commits to one's kin group, ready to sacrifice and put one's self at risk, on the understanding that the others will do the same, and thus collectively all are protected. This spirit of "all for one and one for all" anthropologists call "generalized reciprocity," because returns are not expected from any particular party at any particular time, but rather are expected from any group member when circumstances call for a response. Faith in the other group members is required but, considering the alternative options, it is the best bet, practically speaking.

These three types of motivation contribute to guiding Middle Easterners toward commitment to their kin groups and toward fulfilling their obligations to those groups. However, there is always a difficulty in bridging the gap between the individual's short-term interests and the group's long-term interests. The gap between the individual and group is clear when one group member is injured and killed in consequence of a misdeed by another. The gap between the present and the future is clear when one must pay a heavy indemnity now for a fellow member, with the expectation that some day others might pay on one's behalf. An obvious lack of correspondence is only partly overcome by ideas of duty and conceivable long-term benefits.

Something more is needed to bridge the gap. In the Middle East, particularly the Arab Middle East, the necessary element is a further possibility of extrinsic reward or punishment. This element is the concept of "honor," its presence a recognition of righteous behavior, and a designation of high rank, while its absence is a recognition of failure to fulfill one's duty, and a designation of low rank. Public opinion's judgment of one's actions, as summed in one's reputation, designates one's degree of honor and one's standing among others. In the absence of honor, one is shamed, and one's reputation is in tatters, and one sinks to a low rank. The consequences are serious and can be severe: The willingness of others to work and cooperate with one, and to exchange children in marriage alliances, and ultimately to maintain collective responsibility is based on reputation (Marx 1967: 182–83, 199–200; Lancaster 1997: 46–47, 73, 76, 140; Ginat 1997: ch. 4). Here is the short-term, individual, extrinsic reward and punishment that make actions to support the group in the long run a matter of immediate consequence to the individual. The gap between the individual and the group, and between short-term interest and long-term interest, is bridged. The individual's interest in his honor is manifested in fulfilling his duty for his group, and thus the active commitment of individual members is secured for the group.

However, the quest for honor goes beyond simply doing one's duty and fulfilling one's obligations. For Middle Easterners, the search for honor and the avoidance of shame becomes a goal in its own right. This appears to be an "unintended consequence" of a concept evolved to cement group loyalty. The result is that concerns about honor drive behavior and shape responses. Honor becomes a powerful motivator in social engagement and exchange. Calculations about material interest, and individual and group consequences, never neglect the effects on honor, which often come to outweigh other concerns.

WHERE HONOR LIES

Among Arabs, all men are in principle equal, or, more precisely, not unequal by any prescribed ascription. That is, all men are born equal, without higher or lower rank. It is in this sense that we can say that Arab culture is decisively egalitarian. Each man, being in principle equal to all others, is also in principle autonomous, making decisions for himself according to his own lights. Each man, free to act as he chooses, is thus responsible for his own actions. In this sense, we can say that Arab culture decisively encourages freedom of the individual.

Honor is deemed to reside with those who are able to maintain their equality, independence, and freedom. This is true for both individuals and groups. Subordination of any kind results in a loss of honor, and a sense of shame. Subordination is regarded as a loss of manhood, as manhood and manly virtues—assertiveness, strength, courage, tenacity, endurance, and capability—are equated with honor. As the Arabic proverb puts it, "He who rules over you, emasculates you" (Kressel 1996: 104). Similarly, in any confrontation, conflict, or combat, honor comes with victory and shame comes with defeat. Victory validates manhood and honor, while defeat is symbolic castration and shames the defeated. In the Middle East, in confrontations great and small, there is no virtue in being a victim; there is only the triumph of the victor, and the disgrace of the conquered. Domination gives honor; submission gives shame.

Thus there are, in practice, multiple and ongoing challenges to equality, autonomy, and freedom. Each confrontation, conflict, or combat generates honored victors and shamed losers. This results in different men and groups having differential degrees of honor and shame, and, in ranking these, an achieved hierarchy of honor. Men and their groups may achieve the highest level of independence and the honor that goes with it, but they must assert their claims and struggle for rank. An Arab proverb puts it this way: "Always be sure to claim all due respect for what you have and deserve"(Kressel 1996: 40, note 14). The combination of ascribed equality and achieved hierarchy is what Alexis de Tocqueville found in American democracy: no ascribed status at birth, which resulted in a fierce status competition and a hierarchy of success.

Honor for Arabs and other Middle Easterners is a constant concern and worry, as it is easily challenged and lost. But, at the same time, honor can be increased by timely and effective action, by assertion and courage. In this way, the quest for honor encourages or leads to offensive action, initiatives by individuals or groups against others, for the rewards of honor. Thus relations between individuals and between groups are shaped by the competition for honor. This is no less true for settled and urbanized Arabs as it is for nomadic Bedouin in the desert, no less true for farmers, drivers, wholesalers, and craftsmen as it is for camel herders.

So it was during the thirty years, 1960–1990, between the Barabha, Shalalfa, and Trabelsiyya patrilineal kin groups in the Israeli town of Ramla, eighteen kilometers southeast of Tel Aviv. (I draw here at some length from Gideon M. Kressel's *Ascendancy through Aggression: The Anatomy of a Blood Feud among Urbanized Bedouin*, 1996.) These patrilineages, with Bedouin origins, were part of an Arab population of 3,800 among 30,000 Jews in the town. The members of these lineages, some of whom had lived in the town for decades, had modern occupations in mechanized agriculture, transport, and wholesale commerce. But these lineages tended to live fairly compactly, located in or around the Bedouin quarter and in public housing provided for them. As well, and more important, they maintained their *asabiyya*, their lineage solidarity, and each maintained at least one *shiqq*, a meeting house, for members of the lineage (Kressel 1996: 22–23). This result is not unusual, for, as Kressel (1996: 17) explains, "molding a social landscape of patrilineage quarters . . . [is] the traditional pattern by which urban society in the Middle East has always been structured."

The feud between the lineages began with a small matter, as they often do. An amount of money owed by a Shalalfa to a Barabha led, when they happened to meet, to an exchange of unpleasantries, and the Barabha, some of whose women folk were present, took this as a grave insult, not just to the individual, but to the lineage as a whole (Kressel 1996: ch. 2). (Here we see "in action" the principle of each member standing for all members and for the group as a whole: an insult to one becomes an insult to all.) This exchange became a talking point throughout the two lineages and among the neutral lineages that made up the observing "public."

"Collective responsibility" means that everyone in a lineage is involved in a conflict affecting one of them. As Kressel (1996: 53, note 22) describes the Arab rule,

> Each agnate [male kinsman] is theoretically responsible for avenging injuries [to property, life, and honor] leading back five generations—i.e. to his paternal grandfather's grandfather. What this means in fact is that each agnate is committed to preserving the honor of all living descendants of his paternal great-great-great-grandfather. Should any agnate be injured or insulted, it is the collective responsibility of all the others to take revenge; and in the event that any agnate injures or harms a member of another lineage, he put all of his own *khamsa* ["five," i.e., kin group descended five generations] at risk.

The avoidance or abdication, or even undue postponement of this responsibility, would lead to loss of honor for the group and its members, and bring severe internal criticism upon those not acting.

Then, several days later, the young Shalalfa man who had spoken the insult was ambushed by a number of Barabha youths in the olive grove as he drove his tractor back from work; they had lain in wait for him, stopped him, demanded payment, hit him, and threatened his life. The Shalalfa went to the highest-ranked lineage, the Trabelsiyya, to complain about their injury and hoping to find support for receiving compensation. The Barabha, for their part, claimed that the exchanges were now even, and no one was owed anything. Nor were the Barabha delighted at Trabelsiyya intervention, and were perhaps growing tired of being subordinate in ranking to the leading Trabelsiyya.

Four months later, with angry feelings still simmering in the two lineages, the conflict broke out again. Two of the Barabha drank too much and drove to the Shalalfa houses, where they smashed into one of the Shalalfa cars. The Shalalfa men came out and asked them to stop their attack and go away. The Shalalfa and Barabha men started fighting. The Shalalfa man who had originally passed the insult was stabbed twice, in the head and back of the neck, and taken to the hospital nearly dead. One of the drunk Barabha was knocked on the head with a log by the mother of the stabbed man.

With the advent of serious fighting and major injuries, members of lineages gathered in the *shiqq* meeting rooms along with members of allied smaller lineages to exhibit solidarity. At the same time, Israeli police intervention was initiated, with the goal of stopping the conflict and reinstituting order. The strategy of the police was to add its weight to the traditional Bedouin mediation process (Kressel 1996: 56), which involves first a preliminary cease-fire agreement, called a *wujeh* (literally meaning "face," after the Bedouin notables who agree to act as guarantors of the peace), during which mediators try to work out a formal truce, *'atwa* (literally "gift," the restraint of the injured party), which, with further mediation and negotiation, would lead to a formal reconciliation, *sulh*.

The reports and presentations of the events by the interested parties also develop through phases (Kressel 1996: 59).

First, each side in the fight stresses their own great prowess and the severe injuries that they visited on their opponents. Each side also denies that they themselves suffered any serious injuries. In this phase, each side is trying to bolster its honor by claiming superior strength and denying injury. Even if there is an evident winner and loser—and the judge of this is the public, the other lineages—the losing lineage tries to minimize its loss, just as the winner tries to maximize its victory. The second phase begins with the (informal) public verdict of victor and vanquished. Then, with mediation and compensation looming, the winner asserts its innocence in the conflict, and minimizes the injuries it has caused. The victim now exaggerates its injuries and losses, in order to gain maximum compensation. But of the result for the allocation of honor, for public standing and for the ranking of the lineages, there is no doubt. He who gives compensation is ruled the victor; he who receives compensation is deemed the loser. The victor gains honor; the vanquished loses honor. The victor ranks higher in the hierarchy of honor than the loser.

The Barabha-Shalalfa feud did not, however, move quickly to resolution. The winners in the first encounters, the Barabha, responded arrogantly and refused reconciliation. They went even further, not only refusing to stay hidden and inactive—the urbanized adaptation of the Bedouin moving away until reconciliation—but engaged in a series of celebratory displays, most notably a series of elaborate, expensive, and extended circumcision and wedding festivities. As Kressel (1996: 62) explains, "Conspicuous consumption operated as a kind of 'second front' in what was primarily a violent hierarchical struggle." These festivities served to bring together lineage members and supporters and to both encourage and exhibit *asabiyya*, solidarity.

With the rivalry exacerbated rather than resolved by the delay in resolution procedures and by the competing festivities, both lineages began to build up, to enhance their strength for further confrontation. In a continuation of competitive display, members of both lineages bought motor vehicles and heavy agricultural equipment, and parked them outside their residences. More important, perhaps, was that each lineage was recruiting new local members by attracting relatives from afar through offers of marriage, jobs, modern residence, and, presumably, honor (Kressel 1996: 80). Some new families came from the desert, and merely had to arrive and set up their tents in the vicinity. Three families joined the Barabha, while six joined the Shalalfa.

The negotiations for settlement of the Barabha-Shalalfa dispute continued, but without success. Finally, a month after the end of the celebrations, with no progress in resolution, a Barabha man, a local official hitherto not directly involved in the fighting, was set upon by several Shalalfa, including the man who had been badly stabbed previously, and beaten badly (Kressel 1996: 83–91). Shortly after, some Barabha girls pushed around and shamed a Shalalfa girl with sexual imagery, which heightened tension even more.

Not long after, some Shalalfa who had been living away, as part of the avoidance code required by procedures of mediation, returned to Shalalfa residences. This was observed by some Barabha, who immediately called together Barabha members. A Barabha war party of some forty men and ten women armed with knives and sticks headed to the Shalalfa residence courtyard where, finding no men, they broke many windows. Leaving the residence, they were unexpectedly attacked by around seventy Shalalfa, who easily overcame the Barabha, and who chased them away. The Barabha, surprised and outnumbered, had been decisively defeated by the Shalalfa (Kressel 1996: 96–99). Two Barabha had serious injuries, and nine had slight injuries. It is important to note that injuries, seen perhaps as signs of weakness and defeat, are regarded as shameful, both to the injured person and to his family and lineage. The next day, one of the Barabha, quoting an Arabic proverb, "noted bitterly that 'at the hour of trial a man is either honored or humiliated.'"

It was no accident that the arrival of new recruits acted as reinforcement for the Shalalfa, and that with larger numbers they defeated the Barabha. It is always expected that the lineage with larger numbers will prevail, and that lineage size is equated with power. The larger the size of the lineage, the more warriors, and the lineage with the larger number of warriors is regarded as stronger and likely to be the victor. Larger lineages are thus ranked higher than smaller lineages (Kressel 1996: 105). Rivalries and disputes over honor generally arise, as Kressel (1996: 105) indicates, between "two groups of approximately the same size who occupy adjacent positions on the local hierarchical ladder," each trying to avoid domination by the other, and each hoping to rise over the other. The competition between numerically and hierarchically more or less equivalent lineages reflects the rivalry between equals. But in the end, one prevails and the other loses. Between the Barabha and Shalalfa, the numbers (Kressel 1996: 26, charts 1 and 2) tell the story: When the conflict began, the Barabha counted fifteen nuclear families, while the Shalalfa were only eleven. Four years later, at the culmination of the conflict described, the Shalalfa and allies counted thirty nuclear families, while the Barabha and allies numbered only twenty-three.

The impact on status of numbers is well known from elsewhere in the Middle East. In Cyrenaica (eastern Libya), there is an explicit status distinction between *Hurr*, "the free or noble" tribes, born free and noble as descendants of the founding ancestress, Sa'ada, of the Cyrenaican tribes, who are owners of the land and the water sources, and the *Marabtin*, or clients, who reside and use land and water sources at the pleasure of the free tribes (Peters 1968: 167–68). "A Sa'adi [*Hurr*] tribesman has rights in the country's natural resources which a client cannot claim," says Peters (1968: 171). Each group of client *Marabtin* is "tied" to a free tribe, and will stand with its patron and fight alongside its patron. However, a growth in numbers of a client tribe, or a fall in numbers of a free tribe, can lead to a change in relative status (Peters 1968: 173):

> Less distinguished client groups have grown to outnumber their patron groups, and although the information about their origin is used to discredit them by their debilitated patron groups, they have ceased to be clients in any meaningful sense of the word. In 1948, for example, the aged leader of a small noble group complained bitterly about the number of clients living on his tribal land, but he could not rid himself of them because without them, he and his agnates alone would not constitute a viable corporation; in 1950, these clients announced their intention to water their animals at their patron's well—one of the conventional modes of staking a claim to a piece of territory and the wells in it—and although the patron group threatened the direst opposition, the clients successfully seized the well and the adjacent land. In another tribe, a large group of clients gathered upon a tribal territory, asserted their right to it and beat off an attack by their patrons with guns.

Even the formal status and genealogical place of tribes can change to reflect *fait accompli*. Peters (1968: 172–73) argues that a genealogy is less an accurate record of descent, than a rationalization of actual relations between groups and their territorial relations. Thus a strong and victorious *Marabtin* client group will be incorporated into the genealogy as a free and noble *Hurr* tribe.

> Indeed, the noblest lineage in the whole of the land is reputed to be of client origin, and the tribesmen of this lin-

eage, after recounting the circumstances which permitted their client ancestor to appropriate noblemen's lands, boast their [noble] Sa'adi [genealogical] status. (Peters 1968: 173)

In the desert as well as in urban settlements, a great number of agnates equals military strength, and military strength means practical control, and practical control is recognized in rank and status.

The importance for honor and rank, of numbers of agnates, lineage members, was not lost on the settled, urban-ized Israeli Bedouin making up the Barabha, Shalalfa, Trabel-siyya, and other lineages. Their strategies for increasing the local number of agnates went beyond recruitment of kin from elsewhere and alliances with other lineages. Domestic policies were also designed to increase the number of agnates. Three main strategies served this purpose: First, endogamy, marriage within the lineage, kept the children of daughters in the group. Had the daughters married outside, their children would belong to their fathers' lineages. Second, polygyny, marriage with multiple wives, provided each man with the opportunity to father many children. Third, fathering as many children as possible increased the number of lineage members. We must note, therefore, that the tendency seen elsewhere for decreased fertility as a result of urbanization is not evident here.

Of course, as a result of these strategies, other policies fol-lowed: One was that marriages were arranged for the benefit of the lineage, not necessarily for the preference or satisfaction of the girls. The second was that any woman's preference for monogamy would have to be disregarded in favor of the interest of the lineage. The third was that women were expected to produce as many children as possible, and to look after them. Of course, this would mean that there would be little opportunity to take up extradomestic employment, even leaving aside questions of female shame. The fourth was that fathers had to find ways to support large domestic establish-ments. The fifth was that comfort and ease would have to take second place to the pleasures of a large domestic establishment. The sixth was that the many children had many siblings to con-tend with and a limited possibility of attention from parents.

The *sulh*, or reconciliation between the Barabha and Sha-lalfa, was highly formal and accepted in a very resentful spirit by the fallen Barabha (Kressel 1996: 129–37). The police had insisted on the reconciliation, and the Barabha was in any case in no position to challenge the Shalalfa again. But their loss of honor left their hearts bitter with hatred.

In the following decades, the Barabha successfully built businesses and increased their families. But in 1991, the Barabha challenged the first ranking lineage, the Trabelsiyya (Kressel 1996: 148–55). The Trabelsiyya had aged, and the Barabha had expanded. The outcome was uncertain. Firearms were used and a few people died. The Trabelsiyya suffered more casualties. If they agreed to a truce and accepted com-pensation, they would be admitting that the Barabha had tri-umphed and that the Barabha was ahead of them in the ranking. The Trabelsiyya, originating in Libya, did not think that they could augment their numbers to aid them in this crisis. But media coverage in Israel of this feud led to previ-ously unknown Trabelsiyya living elsewhere in Israel to con-tact them, and thus to augment their numbers. A further con-frontation in 1993 between the Trabelsiyya and Barabha left five Barabha and only one Trabelsiyya injured. Once again, the Barabha had lost, and the Trabelsiyya remained above the Barabha in the ranking.

What conclusions can we draw from the cases examined here? First, that group solidarity, *asabiyya*, and honor, are closely related. Solidarity is supported by the honor of the individual member, and the honor of the group as a whole requires solidarity. Second, that the solidarity that allows the group to defend itself also makes possible offensive action against other groups. Third, that in either defense or offense, military capacity is the decisive factor. Fourth, the number of male agnates determines military capacity. Fifth, that affronts to honor will lead to confrontations, conflicts, and combat. Sixth, competition for places in the honor ranking of groups can lead to confrontations, conflicts, and combat. Seventh, injuries and compensation received signal the loser, and a loss of honor. Eighth, in competitions for honor, there can only be winners and losers. Victors receive honor; the vanquished are humiliated. Domination is always the objective.

While blood feuds appear to be set off by conflicts between individuals, the opposition and rivalry between lineage groups is an underlying structural cause. There are several, apparently conflicting explanations of this group opposition and rivalry. The argument that I have made is that balanced opposition, with its built-in deterrence against attack, arises from the need for security and social control. A second argument, discussed by Kressel (1996: 61), well established in the literature (Lewis 1961; Peters 1960, 1967), is that lineage rivalries and interlineage conflict arise from competition over scarce resources, such as pasture and water in the desert, and, we might add, control over lucrative jobs, trades, or offices in cities. The third position is that of Kressel (1996: 158), who argues that interlineage conflict is over honor:

> Bedouin blood feuds do not revolve around a struggle for scarce material resources. If anything, a considerable outlay is required in order to wage battle. What victory does bring, however, is the intangible benefit of enhanced self-image concomitant with hierarchical status. . . . In a society that values family honor over economic achievements, [greater] deference more than compensates for the lack of material rewards.

These three views appear to suggest that these elements are exclusive, but we must consider whether they refer to distinct, separate streams of causality, which must be reflected in alternative theories of action, or whether the phenomena discussed—security against attack, control of resources, and honor from strength and domination—are different aspects of the same organization and its processes.

It appears to me evident that the desire for security, the quest for resources, and honor, which reflects strength, are all integral aspects of balanced opposition. Another way of putting it is that the quest for lineage independence and dominance is "overdetermined," that is determined by several influences all working in the same direction. Interlineage conflicts arise because people feel that they must defend themselves against all threats, or else become an open target. Interlineage conflicts arise because people feel that they must protect the resources they control and, if possible, expand their control over other resources. Interlineage conflicts arise because people must also defend their honor, which means defending their independence and dominance. Security, control over resources, and honor are different aspects of lineage independence and dominance, and balanced opposition and interlineage conflict involve all three at the same time.

The dynamics of conflict remain the same also at higher levels of integration, such as in sectarian conflicts, and in sophisticated cities far from the deserts: the Shiite–Sunni conflict for domination destroyed Beirut in the 1980s, just as it undermined Karachi at the turn of the millennium, and is washing Baghdad in blood at the time of this writing. Ajami (1999: 121), describing the distinguished Arab poet Adonis, reports "He had seen all the grand ideas and all the ideologies issue in slaughter, and the return of the Lebanese and other Arabs in Lebanon to a primitive tribalism."

WOMEN, HONOR, AND SHAME

Just as honor binds men to the lineage, so too are women bound to the lineage by honor. A woman's behavior reflects on the honor of her family and her lineage. A woman who is modest, obedient, and chaste reflects well on the honor of her family. However, any known immodest behavior, disobedience, or sexual misconduct, which means pre- or extramartial sexual contact, or indeed any apparently intimate contact with nonkin men, shames the woman and her family, which loses honor in the eyes of the public.

The honor at risk from the behavior of women is conceptually somewhat different from the honor at risk in competition between lineages. In competition, whether between individual men, between lineages, or tribes, the type of honor at stake is generally labeled *sharaf*. Ginat (1997: 129; see also Stewart 1994: ch. 4) defines it this way: "*Sharaf* is a type of honor that fluctuates according to a man's behavior. [For example:] If a man looks after the needs of his guests and is seen to be generous to those in need, his honor standing is high. . . . This type of honor can be accumulated or lost according to a man's behavior." Stewart (1994: 59 and ch. 4, passim) refers to this type of honor as "vertical honor": "the right to special respect enjoyed by those who are superior, whether by virtue of their abilities, their rank, their services to the community, their sex, their kin relationship, their office, or anything else."

The other type of honor that is affected by women's behavior is called *'ird*. Ginat (1997: 129) says "*'ird*, on the other hand, is a type of honor that is used 'only in connection with female chastity and continence' [Abou Zeid 1965: 256]. A woman cannot by exemplary conduct add to her agnates' *'ird*, though by misbehaving she can detract from it." For Stewart (1994: 54, 81–85), *'ird* is a kind of "horizontal honor" that he labels "personal honor": "Two features . . . distinguish it from other types: first . . . that [it] can be lost, and second that in order to retain it one must follow certain rules, or maintain certain standards . . ."

Stewart (1994: 83) argues that 'ird, as "personal honor," involves both a man's own behavior and that of his womenfolk.

> The list of actions that dishonor a man [among the Bedouin of Sinai] . . . is short and fairly agreed on. Incomparably the most important in practice is failure to meet the obligations that one takes upon oneself as a guarantor. It is not in general dishonorable for a man to have illegitimate sex relations with a women, but it becomes so when a special relationship of trust has been established, for example, when the man is accompanying the women on a journey, or when the two reside in the same encampment. It is dishonorable to attack one's companion on a journey, or to abandon such companions in a fight. Robbery is not dishonorable, but theft carried out behind the victim's back (e.g. from a cache of grain) is.

'Ird can also be affected by what others do, as Stewart (1994: 109) points out, such as when "someone close to one is treated in a dishonorable way."

> An example occurred among the Bedouin while I was in the field: a young man was alleged to have thrust his hand into the bosom of a young unmarried woman. There was no suggestion that she had offered him even the slightest encouragement. The girl's father received a substantial award from the Manshad [honor court].

The second way in which the behavior of others can affect one's 'ird is if someone close engages in disgraceful behavior, particularly if a woman engages in unsanctioned sexual activity (Stewart 1994: 109). An example of this is a story told in a number of Egyptian oral poems:

> An army sergeant called Mitwalli learns that his sister has
> become a prostitute. He tracks her down, kills her, chops up
> the corpse, and throws it from her balcony to the dogs
> [which are unclean animals for Muslims]. All this is
> described with unqualified approval by the authors of the
> poems, as is Mitwalli's subsequent exoneration in court.

The disgraceful behavior of Mitwalli's sister was a blot on his
honor, and that of his family, and could only be erased by her
blood. In such cases, it is felt that blood cleans humiliation.

Stewart (1994: 83, ch. 5 passim) points out that *'ird* is
"reflexive," by which he means that the original act—whether an
insult to someone closely related, or disgraceful behavior by
someone closely related—does not itself destroy one's honor
irretrievably; it is only by not responding properly to the attack
on one's *'ird* that it will be lost. If a man compensates for a commitment unfulfilled, or cleanses the source of the disgrace—by
punishing or killing the offender—*'ird* is retrieved and restored.
But if, in the eyes of the public, one does not react promptly,
appropriately, and effectively, then one's *'ird* is gone.

The public aspect is essential for shame; the loss of *'ird*, is
a judgment of the public. As a Bedouin judge and mediator
quoted by Ginat (1997: 130) put it, "Shame is not when
someone's daughter has illicit sexual relations; the shame is
when it is public knowledge that she has had illicit sexual relations." Families of course do their best to keep misbehavior
secret, but in face-to-face communities this is very difficult.
Furthermore, as part of *sharaf* honor competition, each family
is watching the others in order to find some advantage for
themselves. An indiscretion by a woman of one family can be
seen by other families as an opportunity to improve their relative positions. As Cohen (quoted in Ginat 1997: 134) puts it,
"An adulterous woman, even an unmarried woman having a
sexual affair with a man, must be killed by her brothers or her

father's brother's sons. If she is killed the group not only reasserts its position but also rises in prestige scale. If she is not killed they suffer loss of prestige." There is thus some interplay between horizontal and vertical honor.

Ginat (1997) has carried out one of the fullest studies of family honor and challenges to 'ird, based upon long-term research (1973–83 and 1986–96) among rural Arabs and Bedouin in Israel. He provides a good number of case studies of the results of women's pre- and extramarital sexual activity. One of his main conclusions is that, while some women are killed and some punished in other ways, others escape severe repercussions. In fact, for every woman who is killed for sexual misbehavior, many more are not. In three communities studied during the period 1988–95 (Ginat 1997: 174–85), of twenty-seven cases of illicit sexual behavior known to the public, three of the women were murdered, while twenty-four received mild punishments or continued their lives undisturbed. Ginat (1997: 187) concludes that

> The case histories presented here show that the ideology which insists on female chastity and female shame as a basic value is by no means invalid. On the other hand, ideology does not rule supreme, and reality creates its own patterns, which are often variations of ideology and compromise solutions. A killing, which does not take place unless there is a public accusation by an injured party, is one form of reacting to the violation of sexual norms, but an extreme one. Sometimes no punishment is imposed nor any sanction; then again, various modes of punishment and sanction may be applied.

Let us examine a few representative cases from an earlier period, to see honor dynamics and the part that lineage standing and lineage politics can play in them.

Case 1 (Ginat 1997: 136). A villager had four daughters by his first wife, and later married a second wife from a respected family of the village. One of the daughters had a love affair with an agricultural worker who came to the village to work. Rumors spread, and when the father heard of this, he arranged for the worker to be fired and thus to disappear from the village.

> His second wife was not satisfied with this solution and reproached her husband for having failed to protect the family honor. She expressed resentment in the presence of members of her natal family who were visiting at the same time and indicated that both her and her husband's status was reduced by his inaction. In reaction to her accusation the father ordered his other daughters to push their sister into the village well at their next daily trip to draw water. This was done and represented as an accident.

It was not the sexual misbehavior that led her father and sisters to kill the girl; rather, it was the public accusation. As Ginat (1997: 136) says, "The father did not kill his daughter when he learned that she had offended the norm. It was his wife's accusation, made in public [i.e., in the presence of her kin], that prompted him to take steps." This circumstance—a public accusation by an injured party, i.e., one who also loses honor—appears, according to Ginat (1997: 136, 187, and *passim*) as a major element, perhaps almost a necessary element, in a murder for sexual misbehavior. Absent such an accusation, murder rarely if ever takes place.

Case 2 (Ginat 1997: 141–45). In a case that became famous in Israel, due to subsequent media coverage and legal appeals, a girl from a Triangle Region village became pregnant and identified a young man of her lineage as her lover. He was already engaged to be married with a father's brother's daughter in a complicated exchange of brides between two close families, a commitment that proved to be difficult to break. So the violation could not be resolved by a marriage of the lovers, a preferred solution to such a problem. The father of the young man promised that a younger son would marry the girl immediately after the exchange wedding. But the young brother refused, and the girl's family was left with no solution. Rumors spread in the village about the girl. Relations between the families became strained. After six months, with no resolution in sight, an uncle and the girl's brother agreed to strangle her, but were talked out of it by a senior member of the lineage. After a year, on quite a separate matter, the girl's family was unexpectedly insulted.

> The girl's mother reacted to what she considered an insult added to injury with a hysterical accusation of her husband, calling his handling of the whole affair incompetent and charging him with indifference. She shouted that "First they lay our daughter and then they want to devour us," and so loud was her voice that she was heard by some of the neighbors. The upset father's reaction was immediate. He picked up a hoe, entered the room where the girl was sleeping, and hit her over the head until she was dead.

In cases 1 and 2, the injured party who makes the accusation is the wife, and thus a member of the immediate family. But it is also common for members of the wider family, of the lineage, to make such accusations.

Case 3 (Ginat 1997: 148–49). Warda, a Druze woman from a Galilee village, who had lived in the United States for several years, returned from time to time to visit her family. She dressed immodestly like Western women, paraded around the village, and sometimes spent the evening and even the night away. Gossip about her spread through the village, and it was said that she was associating with a Jew. Her brother

Suhail, who was in the Israeli army, did not interfere. But one day

> Suhail came home on leave from the army base where he was serving, and as he reached the house his uncle shouted to him: "Your only concern is that your uniform should be ironed, while I tear my clothes out of shame." He added, "Not only does she do what she does, she flaunts her immoral behavior by also wearing earrings." These angry words were heard by neighbors. . . . Several hours after the uncle remonstrated against this, Suhail shot and killed his sister.

It is common for such accusations to come from relatives whose honor is also besmirched, such as uncles and cousins.

Case 4 (Ginat 1997: 149–50). Mahmud, believing his wife, Leila, unfaithful with a man she had wanted to marry, pretended to go on a trip, and caught his wife and her lover in intimate relations. The lover ran away, and Mahmud threw Leila out, sending her to her parents' house, and arranged to show the clothes of the lovers to Leila's father, Moussa, and her brothers.

> [Moussa's] sons and nephews . . . insisted that the disgrace be wiped clean [by Leila's blood], yet Moussa prevaricated, until one day a nephew shouted from the balcony of his house that he intended to exile himself from the village, as he was so ashamed that he could no longer walk the streets or look anyone in the eye. Only then did Moussa kill his daughter.

As with many such cases in Israel, the killer is arrested, sent to trial, and given a long sentence, not uncommonly life in prison, in accordance with Israeli law. And, as with many such cases, the prisoner appeals to the authorities for leniency.

Moussa's letter to the President of Israel, asking for amnesty, states that he never actually wanted to kill his daughter, and that he recognizes that he lives in the twentieth century, and that despite all the disgrace and pain he had no wish to blot out the shame with murder. But as he explains in his letter, he had no choice—he was pushed to do it by his family.

Ginat thus makes a strong case for his thesis, that honor killings take place not as a result of norm violation, but as a consequence of a public denunciation by an affected party.

There is, however, another dimension that is elicited by Ginat, a political dimension. In case 5 (Ginat 1997: 137–38) a Negev girl had abandoned her newborn, and, once discovered, identified her young lover, whose family would not agree to a marriage. The families parted when the girl's family migrated. But

the girl's uncles were obviously dissatisfied and one of them repeatedly accused her father of neglecting the problem, insisting that he clear the family name. Not long afterwards the girl's body was found at the bottom of a well.

But there was more to this than honor, as Ginat (1997: 138) explains:

Political motives also enter the picture in that the girl's uncle, who appeared eager to defend the family honor, had an ulterior motive. He wished to use the girl's murder [or, more accurately: cleansing the girl's dishonorable deed and the reputation of the lineage] as a means of uniting his co-liable group, the sheikh of which had died several years previously. Since that time the cohesion of the co-liable group had been on the decline. A murder [cleansing] would thus rally them together.

As well, in case 2, described above, there was a political motive. One of the uncles of both the girl and the boy lovers spread rumors of the girl's impurity and the boy's guilt, which led to the affair being public knowledge in the community. He even went so far as to accuse and even assault his nephew, the boy lover, in public. While concern about the honor of the lineage was a motive, it was not the only one (Ginat 1997: 144):

> It was known that [the uncle] wanted the young man's position and standing in the community, and even more the position of his father, to be reduced for political reasons. This, of course, had nothing to do with the girl and her conduct. The aim of the uncle was to ostracize them and to oust them from the group, the motivation for which dated back to an earlier time when there had been antagonism between himself and the young man's father. This latent hostility was fanned by what had happened and an opportunity was used to settle old accounts.

It appears, according to Ginat's cases, that people's actions reflect a combination or interplay of several motives. When more than one motive pushes in a particular direction, we can say, following the psychologists, that the actions were "overdetermined." Ginat (1997: 187) makes this clear when he says that "ideology does not rule supreme, and reality creates its own patterns, which are often variations of ideology and compromise solutions." Sometimes other motives block what ideology would demand; other times other motives strengthen what ideology demands; and yet other times other motives go beyond what ideology would demand.

The political motives exhibited in cases 2 and 5 also show the imperatives of balanced opposition, but at different levels of organization. In case 2, the political motive shows there is the opposition between man and man, or nuclear family vs.

nuclear family. In case 5, the political motive aims to unify the co-liable or fifth-generation lineage, as a precaution for anticipated opposition with other co-liable lineages.

HONOR AND BALANCED OPPOSITION

In all societies, there is, at the very least, an esteem hierarchy that differentially ranks individuals and groups according to how well they fulfill the norms (Parsons 1954: ch. 4; Fallers 1973: ch. 1). One universal aspect of social life is a competition among constituent individuals and groups for prestige, a competition that requires ever more exemplary fulfilling of norms, or at least convincing public opinion of such exemplary fulfilling. Competing individuals and groups strive to improve or at least maintain their ranking in relation to others. One strategy for rank competition is increasing fulfillment of the norms: making oneself or one's group more religious, or richer, or purer, or militarily stronger, or more creative, or whatever the norms require. Another strategy is to undermine one's competitors, making them, or at least making them appear to be less religious, poorer, more polluted, militarily weaker, uncreative, and so on.

Rank competition is exacerbated in the Middle East, because the main organizational structure is balanced opposition between groups. The competition for esteem corresponds and is confounded with the competition between security defense groups, at all levels: individual, family, lineage, section, tribe, tribal confederacy, sect, religion. Rank competition is commonly manifested between security groups in terms of military strength (which, as we have seen, more or less corresponds to number of warriors).

The impact of female purity or impurity, female shame, on the honor of men also has a strong influence on esteem status of individuals and groups. How can we explain the existence of rules for female purity—the necessity for female obedience, modesty, chastity? The answer I believe is that women's reproductive capacity is necessary for lineage strength, and therefore the ability of the lineage to allocate women where they are needed most for strategic purposes, whether endogamously to contribute to the number of offspring, or exogamously to establish or maintain an alliance, whether monogamously or polygynously, requires an emphasis on obedience. Women must marry where they are needed for lineage strength. Second, the necessity of knowing that lineage offspring truly continue the descent line, which is deemed the defining basis of the group, and therefore are the offspring of legitimate lineage consorts, requires in women modesty and chastity, the former being the overt display of the latter. As well, control of women, just as control of men, indicates internal lineage control and unity, and as such is an indication of strength.

The close attention of community members to the sexual behavior of women reflects not only a concern for fulfilling community norms, "behaving decently," and not only a prurience about forbidden behavior, but also a keen self-interest in rank competition, and the ways in which different groups may be tending to rise or fall. Ultimately public opinion is the judge, so observers from the public are also actors, as communicators and judges.

For men, honor follows strength; lineages that are large and militarily strong are highly regarded and seen as important, while lineages that are small and militarily weak are seen as low and dismissed as unimportant. Gaining strength and proving one's competitors weaker raises one's rank. Deliberate strategies and tactics are employed to advance one's group. Recruiting new members, increasing offspring, building a stock of equipment and weaponry, and making alliances are tried and true strategies for increasing lineage strength. Undermining other groups directly, either through neutralizing or attracting allies of other groups, or even seducing their women, are not unknown (although this latter is not well documented).

Individuals, families, lineages (including the Arab five generation co-liable group, or *khamsa*), tribal sections, tribes, and so forth, not only try to maintain their balance against their opponents, but also try to improve their position against their opponents. In this sense, everyone is universally implicated in political life throughout the Arab world and the Middle East in general, and political life is a continual struggle, with security and rank at stake.

Honor, which I argue developed to support the lineage through tying individual short-term interests to lineage long-term interests and through controlling female fertility, has become a factor and influence in its own right. This is of course normal for cultural mechanisms: cultural means evolve into cultural ends. To be honorable is an end in itself. Now honor itself is worthy of sacrifice in its own right, and of even the ultimate sacrifice.

Chapter 5

TURNING TOWARD THE WORLD
Tribal Organization and Predatory Expansion

A s we have seen, Middle Eastern tribal organization, structured by balanced opposition, serves impressively in making a living through pastoralism and in defending life and property. But the efficacy of balanced opposition does not end there. The third main sphere of its success is external, in increased control over other people and their resources. Tribal solidarity and balanced opposition have been and are powerful means of predatory expansion (Sahlins 1961).

The principle "ally with the closer against the more distant" applies not only within the tribe but outside as well. Just as all members of a small lineage are obliged to unify and support the lineage against another lineage, all members of a tribe are expected to unify and support the tribe in conflict with members of other tribes or other peoples. This does not necessarily mean that all members of the tribe automatically line up in one gigantic regiment, but rather that other members of the tribe will see themselves as unified against the outsiders, and will be inclined to provide material support if and when necessary.

DEMOGRAPHY AND EXPANSION

Among tribal peoples, external geographical and political expansion receives a push from internal demographic expansion, the increase of human and animal population. Nothing is so desired by tribesmen as many children and many livestock. There are very good, practical reasons for this. The first reason for having many children is the need for many hands in production. Labor is one of the main inputs for increasing production. Nomadic pastoralism under preindustrial conditions is highly labor intensive. That is, there is a great deal of physical work, often involving shifting heavy animals, equipment, and supplies around. Furthermore, there are many distinct, and in many cases, spatially separated activities that need attention at the same time but in different places. Ideally, different people would be available to oversee or undertake those activities. As well, because members of the family have common interests, they are deemed to be more reliable in pursuing tasks for the benefit of the family, than are other individuals that might be recruited for reciprocity or pay.

The second reason for having many children is that political and military standing and power is dependent upon the number of individual fighters supporting you, as we have seen in the previous chapter. In the political context, the equivalent of many hands is many strong arms. In preindustrial conditions, military technology is modest, and the main factor in military strength is the number of individuals mobilized. Of course the fighters' skill, condition, and motivation is also critical. But among tribesmen, we can assume that these are more or less equivalent across the board, and thus numbers become the main factor. The man who can call on five or six adult sons and a similar number of sons-in-law to support him is a strong man. This nucleus of power would serve as a magnet, drawing others somewhat more distant, such as cousins, and a power center develops. Thus a man with many children is more likely to be strong and less likely to be vulnerable than others with fewer supporters.

As we have said, one of the main motivations for engaging in polygyny is the desire for many children. Polygyny is particularly called for if a first union is sterile. A man will hope that the problem is with his wife, and that another wife will be fertile and produce children. Another problem is the high rate of miscarriage, stillbirth, and infant and child mortality. This means that survival of children is low, and perhaps two births are required for one child to survive to adulthood. There is also a life cycle periodicity to the need for children. Children really become useful economically from age ten until they marry, in the teens for females and early twenties for males. Once married, a couple has their own economic establishment separate from their parents. So all children are not effective workers throughout their lives. Many children are thus needed so that those who marry and set up their own households can be replaced by those becoming old enough to be helpful in household tasks.

The practical reasons for having many children are signaled symbolically by values and cultural judgments. A man is not a man if he cannot produce children. Impotence in fertility indicates impotence in male strength. This is basic to a man's identity. In a parallel way, a woman fulfills herself by being a mother and is not really an adult until she becomes a mother. For both men and women, children are a great gift and the subject of the fullest affection and closest attention. People are not shy to say that their children are what they value most.

There are equally good reasons to have lots of livestock. Livestock are best understood as capital that produce a good income of offspring and products and services. The milk that camels, sheep, and goats produce, drunk sweet or soured, or transformed into butter or dried milk solids, is a major foodstuff packed with protein and other nutrients. Surplus animals, usually extra males or old females, are occasionally slaughtered for meat, and skins and other parts are important raw materials. Camels offer hair and wool, sheep supply wool, and goats provide underwool and hair: wool is spun into yarn and woven into camel bags, saddle bags, storage bags, food covers, meal rugs, prayer rugs, and sitting rugs; goat hair is spun into yarn and woven into sheets used as tent roofs. Yes, the livestock provide both food and housing (Salzman 2000)! But even this is just the beginning.

Camels are ridden for distance travel, such as for shopping in a distant market, migrating to a distant site, or predatory raiding and warfare. Camels are also burden animals, carrying heavy loads of household goods, supplies, or raw material. Actually there are many varieties of camels: some fine and fast ones used exclusively for riding, and other more robust varieties used for burden. Describing these varieties is an elaborate vocabulary of camel-classification terms (Salzman 2000: 103).

Livestock are also slaughtered for ritual sacrifice, primarily to celebrate religious holy days.

In the Middle East, you can never have too many livestock, not so much for the livestock itself, but for what you do with it. In this sense, livestock is rather like money. One thing you can do is use livestock for marriage, as the rights over children are exchanged for compensation to the woman's kin, and the compensation has traditionally been livestock. From a wife or wives come children, so very good for all of the reasons outlined above. Another thing you can do with livestock is provide hospitality for guests, a major source of honor for the host and also his group. Any man with political aspirations must provide hospitality for many guests, and this requires the means, which are primarily livestock (Lancaster 1997). A third thing you can do is reinforce or establish alliances by loaning or giving livestock to other families. This puts them in a position of obligation to you and their honor is at stake in fulfilling their obligation, usually offered in labor or political support. A fourth thing you can do is sell livestock in markets for money to be used for buying items not available locally, such as firearms, brass household goods, fine carpets, tea, and sugar (Barth 1961: 98). Many livestock can provide funds sufficient to buy agricultural land, peasant villages, and urban villas, which are favorite investments for tribal elites (Barth 1961: 104–11).

It is thus part of the job description for Middle Eastern tribesmen to maximize the number of their children and the number of their livestock. To the extent that they are successful, both the human and animal population expands. Now if the increase in the human and animal populations is the result of intratribal processes of reproduction and production, there will be increased pressure on tribal resources of water, pasture, space, and so on, to accommodate and support the enlarged populations, and thus pressure to expand tribal resources through geographical expansion, at the expense of neighboring populations, if necessary.

Alternatively, in order to speed up the process of increase, the equation can be turned around: geographical expansion at the expense of neighbors through predatory raiding or conquest can lead to increase in herds by capture, and to control over additional territory with pasture and water resources. This strategy is particularly attractive to intrepid young tribesmen who see it as a quick way to independence and prominence (Lancaster 1997).

The desire for an increase of people and livestock thus

leads tribesmen to look outward, beyond their boundaries and to think of expansion at the expense of their neighbors. Let us remember that because of their way of life tribesmen are hardy, and because of their reliance on self-help, tribesmen are ready and able to fight. And because of their tribal structure of balanced opposition, tribesmen feel themselves unified against outsiders, and accept as natural an antipathy between themselves and any other tribe. Challenging neighbors over territory and livestock seems entirely natural and justified, as well as highly desirable.

The modus operandi of predatory expansion is raiding, with the capture of livestock being the first priority. Attacks on the human population tend to vary according to the cultural distance of the outsiders. Those close are treated with some consideration: men are allowed to escape and women are not harmed, nor is housing destroyed. Among Bedouin, women from other Bedouin groups are often left some mulch animals to support their children (Sweet 1965; Irons 1965; Lancaster 1997: 141). But resistance is met by force, and injuries or deaths lead to blood feuds. Tribes can respond to blood feuds with large parties bent on vengeance. Conflict can thus escalate, mobilizing greater numbers and leading to direct confrontation and all-out battle. Losers can escape by retreat, taking their household and livestock with them. This leaves the territory open for occupation by the winners, who have no difficulty expanding into their new area.

The concept of "honor" is relevant to raiding and predatory expansion. Honor in Middle Eastern tribal culture is won in a number of ways concordant with tribal values: First, honor is won by fulfilling one's obligations according to the dictates of lineage solidarity and balanced opposition. Second, honor is won by neutral mediators who succeed in resolving conflicts and reinstituting peaceful relations among tribesmen. Third, and most relevant here, honor is won by succeeding in conflict between lineages in opposition. Violence against outsiders is a well-established path for those seeking honor. But attempts do not bring honor. Success brings honor. Winners gain honor; losers lose honor. In Middle Eastern tribal culture, victims are not celebrated, but generally despised.

Nothing is more common in the history of tribes in the Middle East and North Africa than battles between tribes, the displacement of one by another, the pushing of losing tribes out of their territories. Sometimes losing tribes must become dependents of stronger tribes, which allow them access to territory. Sometimes, losing tribes must retreat to peasant areas, such as the Nile Valley, and are absorbed into the peasantry, losing also their tribal nature (Evans-Pritchard 1949; Peters 1990).

THE RISE OF ISLAM

What was extraordinary in Middle Eastern history was the unification of the Arabian tribes under the banner of Islam and their conquest of much of the known world. Prior to Muhammad, the tribes of northern Arabia engaged in ongoing raiding and feuding, fighting among themselves for the spoils of livestock, territory, and honor. Muhammad's genius was in finding a way to unite the myriad of fissiparous, feuding Bedouin tribes of northern Arabia into a cohesive polity. Just as he had provided a constitution of rules under which the people of Medina could live together, so he also provided a constitution for all Arabs; but this one had the imprimatur not just of Muhammad, but of God. Submission—*islam*—to God and his rules, spelled out in the Koran, bound into solidarity Arabian tribesmen, who collectively became the *umma*, the community of believers.

Building on the tribal system of balanced opposition, Muhammad was able to frame an inclusive structure within which the tribes had a common, God-given identity as Muslim. Their common identity gave the tribes a common interest and common project. But unification was only possible by extending the basic tribal principle of balanced opposition. This Muhammad did by opposing the Muslim to the infidel, and the *dar al-Islam*, the land of Islam and peace, to the *dar al-harb*, the land of the infidels and conflict. Balanced opposition was raised to a higher structural level, and the newly Muslim tribes were unified in the face of the infidel enemy. Bedouin raiding was thus sanctified as an act of religious duty.

With every successful battle against unbelievers, especially after the critical early battle against the Meccans, more Bedouin joined the *umma*. Once united, the Bedouin warriors of the *umma* turned outward, teaching the world the meaning of *jihad*, holy war. The rest, as they say, is history.

The Arabs, in lightning thrusts, challenged and beat the Byzantines to the north and the Persians to the east, both weakened by their continuous wars with one another, thus imposing their control over the Christian majority in the Levant and the Zoroastrian majority in Persia, and therefore over the entire Middle East. These stunning successes were rapidly followed by conquests of Christian and Jewish populations in Egypt, Libya, and the Maghreb (Arabic for "the West"), and, in the East, central Asia, and the Hindu population in northern India. Not content with these triumphs, Arab armies invaded and subdued much of Christian Spain and Portugal, and all of Sicily. Since the Roman Empire, the world had not seen such power and reach. All, almost all, fell before the Saracen blades.

Conquest of vast lands, large populations, and advanced civilizations is bound to be a bloody and brutal task. This is true of all great invasions, including those of the Greek, Roman, Arab, Mongol, Russian, British, Dutch, French, and

Zulu empires, and more recently the short-lived ones of the German and Japanese empires, as well as the campaigns to defeat those empires. Of course some campaigns and occupations are known to have been particularly and gratuitously savage and cruel.

Now we must touch on the nature of the Islamic conquests, not from a prurience for violence, or a desire to condemn Arabs or Muslims, but to clarify an obscure and obfuscated history that demonstrates and illuminates attitudes and relations. This is necessary because it is common for university students and nonspecialists, well indoctrinated with the mantra "Islam is the religion of peace," to ask whether—these are quotes from advanced students—"anything bad really happened" or "anyone got hurt" during the Islamic conquests of most of the civilized world. Most accounts of Islamic history, even that of Lindholm's (2002: 79) esteemed work, glide over the conquests, as if they were friendly takeovers, really to everyone's satisfaction:

> After the death of Muhammad in 632 expansion was rapid; in 638 Jerusalem fell, and in the next thirty years all of ancient Mesopotamia, Egypt and most of Iran were conquered, while other Muslim armies pressed north–west into Byzantine territory. . . . [This] miraculously solved the old regional problem of economic and political impasse by forcibly dissolving the two competing deadlocked opponents [Byzantium and Persia] into Islamdom, abruptly uniting the Middle East into one open trade area and paving the way for the rapid creation of a new prosperity. At the same time, the Muslim message of the equality of all believers struck a cord with the common people of the empires, who, theoretically at least, were liberated from their inferior status by the simple act of conversion. The rise of Islam was both an economic and social revolution, offering new wealth and freedom to the dominions it assimilated

under the banner of a universal brotherhood guided by the message of the Prophet of Allah.

Yes, no doubt it was the best of all possible worlds; that is if one had not been one of the multitude slain, the myriads enslaved, or the remainder expropriated, suppressed, and degraded.

Fortunately there are some accounts we can turn to for franker accounts of the Islamic conquests. Bostom (2005: 141–248) provides lengthy quotes from major Islamic authorities, ancient and modern, verifying the obligation of *jihad*, or holy war against infidels, for every Muslim. Historical accounts are then provided (Bostom 2005: 383–674; see also Holt, Lambton, and Lewis 1970; Cook 2005; and Karsh 2006) of *jihad* campaigns in all parts of the world. A few illustrations will suffice.

An article on Greek Christian accounts of *jihad*, by Demetrios Constantelos (in Bostom 2005: 390), reports the following:

> John of Nikiu speaks of the early invasion of the Arabs in Egypt as merciless and brutal. Not only did the invaders slay the commander of the Byzantine troops and all his companions when they captured the city of Bahnasa, but "they put to the sword all that surrendered, and they spared none, whether old men, babes, or women." They perpetrated innumerable acts of violence and spread panic everywhere.

Constantelos continues:

> When [the Arabs] took the city of Daras (640) by storm, they put many of the inhabitants to the sword. Caesarea in Palestine had a similar fate. After seven years of siege, the Arabs captured the city in 643 and put to death 7,000 Greeks. Cyprus was ravaged when it fell to the Arabs in 650, and the small city of Arados on the island of Arados was totally destroyed by fire in 651 and its walls demolished. Those of

the inhabitants who did not meet death were forced to evacuate the island. . . . Other towns and villages were either sacked or depopulated.

Religious institutions were a favored target (Constantelos in Bostom 2005: 393):

> Greek sources of the eighth century speak also of the savagery of Saracen robbers who raided various monasteries, killing and plundering. For example, during the caliphate of Harun al-Rashid (786–809), the monasteries of Palestine suffered from numerous raids. Many monks were put to death. The monastery of St. Sabbas was invaded in 786 and several monks were slaughtered. . . .
> . . . A Muslim historian reports that over 30,000 churches "which had been built by Greeks" were destroyed in Egypt, Syria, and elsewhere.

About the Armenian rebellion of 703 reported by Aram Ter-Ghevondian (in Bostom 2005: 412), the Arab historian Yaqubi (died 897) wrote,

> [General Muhammad-ibn-Marwan] invaded Armenia whose population had rebelled. He massacred, enslaved and wrote a letter to the nobility who are called freemen, gave guarantees and promised to give honors. Hence they gathered in their churches, in the province of Khlat (Khram) and he ordered to encircle the churches with fire-wood, closed the doors on them and burnt all of them.

Here was a foreshadowing of the Turkish and Kurdish *jihad* genocide of the Armenians in the second decade of the twentieth century (Bostom 2005: ch. 43).

Muslim occupiers of southern Spain, the allegedly "tolerant" civilization of Al-Andalus, are advised in the late fourteenth century by the Grenadan Ibn Hudayl (Bostom 2005: 419–20) that

> It is permissible to set fire to the lands of the enemy, his stores of grain, his beasts of burden—if it is not possible for the Muslims to take possession of them—as well as to cut down his trees, to raze his cities, in a word, to do everything that might ruin and discourage him, . . . suited to hastening the Islamization of that enemy or to weakening him. Indeed, all this contributes to a military triumph over him or to forcing him to capitulate.

In fact, only Muslim dominance is tolerated, and any means of extending it to new lands is sanctioned and sanctified. (Documentation challenging any notion of internal "tolerance" in Islamic Spain is presented in Bostom [2005: 57–60]. See also Littman and Ye'or [2005: 93], quoted below.)

One of the main characteristics of the Arab Empire was the enslavement of conquered peoples (Bostom 2005: 86–93). During conquest, men were commonly slaughtered, while women and children were taken into slavery. Men who willingly converted were spared, but their wives and children were taken as slaves. In conquered regions, children were regularly taken from parents, while on the borders—especially in central and eastern Europe, central Asia, and Africa south of the Sahara—raiding for slaves was normal practice. Of the male slaves, a substantial number were made eunuchs by the removal of sex organs, in order to serve in harems. The women and children were used as domestic and sex slaves.

The Arab campaign in northern India illustrates the usual procedures (Lal in Bostom 2005: 549–50):

> During the Arab invasion of Sindh (712 CE), Muhammad bin Qasim first attacked Debal, a word derived from *Deval*

meaning temple. It was situated on the seacoast not far from modern Karachi. It was garrisoned by four thousand Kshatriya soldiers and served by three thousand Brahmans. All males of the age of seventeen and upwards were put to the sword and their women and children were enslaved. "[Seven hundred] beautiful females, who were under the protection of Budh (that is, had taken shelter in the temple), were all captured with their valuable ornaments, and clothes adorned with jewels." Muhammad dispatched one-fifth of the legal spoil to Hajjaj which included seventy-five damsels, the other four-fifths were distributed among soldiers. Thereafter whichever places he attacked like Rawar, Sehwan, Dhalila, Brahmanabad, and Multan, Hindu soldiers and men with arms were slain, the common people fled, or, if flight was not possible, accepted Islam, or paid the poll tax, or died with their religion. Many women of the high class immolated themselves in Jauhar, most others became prize of the victors. These women and children were enslaved and converted, and batches of them were despatched to the Caliph in regular installments. For example, after Rawar was taken Muhammad Qasim "halted there for three days during which he massacred , (men). Their followers and dependents, as well as their women and children were taken prisoner. Later on "the slaves were counted, and their number came to 60,000. . . . Out of these, 30 were young ladies of the royal blood. . . . Muhammad Qasim sent all these to Hajjaj" who forwarded them to Walid the Khalifa. "He sold some of these female slaves of royal birth, and some he presented to others." Selling of slaves was a common practice. . . .

In Sindh female slaves captured after every campaign of the marching army were converted and married to Arab soldiers who settled down in colonies established in places like Mansura, Kuzdar, Mahfuza, and Multan. . . . In the final states of the conquest of Sindh, "when the plunder and the prisoners of war were brought before Qasim . . . one-fifth of all the prisoners were chosen and set aside; they were

counted as amounting to twenty thousand in number . . .
(they belonged to high families) and veils were put on their
faces, and the rest were given to the soldiers." Obviously a
few *lakh* (hundreds of thousands) were enslaved in the
course of Arab invasion of Sindh.

The Arab conquest of the Sindh was followed by the Afghan
Ghaznavid conquests (Lal in Bostom 2005: 550–52):

> If such were the gains of the "mild" Muhammad bin Qasim
> in enslaving . . . in Sindh, the slaves captured by Mahmud of
> Ghazni, "that ferocious and insatiable conqueror," of the
> century beginning with the year 1000 CE have of course to
> be counted in hundreds of thousands. . . . When Mahmud
> Ghaznavi attacked Waihind in 1001–1002, he took 500,000
> persons of both sexes as captive. This figure [is] of Abu Nasr
> Muhammad Utbi, the secretary and chronicler of Mahmud.
> . . . Next year from Thanesar, according to Farishtah, "the
> Muhammadan army brought to Ghaznin 200,000 captives
> so that the capital appeared like an Indian city, for every sol-
> dier had several slaves and slave girls. . . . The Tarikh-i-Alfi
> adds that the fifth share due to the Saiyyads was 150,000
> slaves, therefore the total number of captives comes to
> 750,000. . . . In every campaign of Mahmud large-scale mas-
> sacres preceded enslavement. . . . Not only were the captives
> physically tortured, they were also . . . systematically humili-
> ated and exposed to public ridicule.

The multitude of reports from Muslim, indigenous, and other
sources of the Islamic conquests are equally detailed and
equally daunting to a modern reader. The reports provided
above are sufficient to remind us of their true nature.

MUSLIMS VS. INFIDELS

How did the Arabs conceive and perceive other peoples, cultures, and societies? What was their understanding of other lives? For the newly minted Muslims, Islam was God's word and God's way, and any other religion or belief was regarded as false. Judaism and Christianity were seen as superseded by Islam, and inferior and degraded remnants. All non-Muslims were infidels, and should be subject to Islam, God's way. Jews and Christians were to be allowed to live as inferiors and subordinates, *dhimmi*, under Muslim domination, but with obligatory, legally mandated humiliation; other infidels, such as Zoroastrians, Hindus, and pagans, were given the choice between conversion to Islam and death. In practice, however, slavery of infidels was often more attractive to the Muslim conquerors, so some infidels were allowed to live enslaved lives of degradation and service to Muslims.

The reader may find this characterization of relations between Muslims and infidels harsh and uncongenial. We have repeatedly been told of the tolerance that existed in the Muslim world, and of the flourishing of minorities under the enlightened guidance of Islamic law and Muslim rulers. But the historical evidence for a darker picture is overwhelming and irrefutable. It is true that, throughout history, intergroup relations in most of the world were exploitative and repressive, and not infrequently brutal and bloodthirsty. The world of Islam was not so much an exception to this, as exemplary of it.

ISLAM MUST DOMINATE

The theological foundation of the Arab Empire was the supremacy of Islam and the obligation of each Muslim to advance its domination. Ye'or (2002: 40–41) sums this point as follows:

> The general basic principles according to the Koran are as
> follows: the pre-eminence of Islam over all other religions
> (9: 33); Islam is the true religion of Allah (3: 17) and it
> should reign over all mankind (34: 27); the *umma* [commu-
> nity of Muslims] forms the party of Allah and is perfect (3:
> 106), having been chosen above all peoples on earth it alone
> is qualified to rule, and thus elected by Allah to guide the
> world (35: 37). The pursuit of *jihad* [holy war], until this
> goal will be achieved, is an obligation (8: 40). [Citations in
> the text refer to the Koran. Comments in brackets added.]

The relationship between Muslims and non-Muslims is thus
defined by Islamic doctrine as one of superiority–inferiority,
and of endless conflict until the successful conquest of the
non-Muslims. As Ye'or (2002: 43) explains,

> *Jihad* divides the peoples of the world into two irreconcilable
> groups: the Muslims—inhabitants of the *dar al-Islam*,
> regions subject to Islamic law; and infidels [*kafir*]—inhabi-
> tants of the *dar al-harb* (*harbis*), the territory of war, destined
> to come under Islamic jurisdiction, either by the conversion
> of its inhabitants or by armed conflict. *Jihad* is the Muslim's
> permanent state of war or hostility by the *dar al-Islam* against
> the *dar al-harb*, until the infidels' conclusive submission and
> the absolute world supremacy of Islam.

Ye'or (2002: 43–47) substantiates this generalization with
quotes from Muslim sources. I include one here, from Ibn
Taymiya, a famous Hanbali jurist of the fourteenth century:

> In ordering *jihad* Allah has said: "Fight them until there is no
> persecution and religion becomes Allah's". [2: 189]
>   Allah has, in fact, repeated this obligation [to fight] and
> has glorified *jihad* in most of the Medina *suras*: he has stig-
> matized those who neglected to do so, and treated them as
> hypocrites and cowards.

> . . . *Jihad* is the best form of voluntary service that man
> consecrates to Allah.
>
> Therefore, since *jihad* is divinely instituted, and its goal is
> that religion reverts in its entirety to Allah and to make
> Allah's word triumph, whoever opposes the realization of
> this goal will be fought, according to the unanimous
> opinion of Muslims. (Quoted in Ye'or 2002: 44)

Any male infidel who resists Islamic domination may be killed
or enslaved; women and children must be taken into slavery
(Ye'or 2002: 44–45).

We may ask whether the doctrinal views of the fourteenth
century are outdated, or whether they have been carried down
to the present day. Here anthropologists have a contribution to
the discussion. E. E. Evans-Pritchard, late professor of social
anthropology at Oxford University, had close contact with the
Bedouin of Libya during World War II, and, as reported in his
brilliant account, *The Sanusi of Cyrenaica* (1949: 63), the
Bedouin saw it as their special religious responsibility to carry
out holy war, *jihad*, leaving others to pray and study the Koran.
When Libya was invaded by the Italians early in the twentieth
century, the Bedouin of Cyrenaica (the eastern half of Libya)
were unwilling to accept the Italians as rulers under any terms,
no matter how generous. Although the Bedouin were heavily
outgunned, they chose to fight and continued to fight coura-
geously for decades until they were virtually exterminated.

While *jihad* must never be terminated until Islam is universal and all follow Allah's way, a break in military hostilities
is lawful. An-Nawawi, Shafi'i jurisconsult of the thirteenth century (quoted in Ye'or 2002: 46) said,

> An armistice is only allowed when some advantage to Mus-
> lims ensures: for example, if we are weak in numbers, or if we
> lack money or ammunition, or even if there is hope that the

infidels may convert or offer to surrender and pay the capitation tax. . . . On the other hand, it is perfectly lawful for the sovereign, when he agrees to an armistice, to reserve the right to recommence hostilities when it seems good to him.

Strategic pauses are thus sanctioned, as long as the obligation to continue the *jihad* is honored.

THE WORLD WAS MADE BY ALLAH AND BELONGS TO MUSLIMS

The Islamic dominance of the world extends to all material aspects of the world. Allah made the world, and thus Muslims, as the true followers of Allah, have a right to all that Allah made. As Ye'or (2002: 44) describes,

Because the Islamic community is sanctified by possession of the only true religion, it is also the only legitimate beneficiary of the material wealth created by Allah. Thus *jihad*, which strives to "restore" to Muslims the possession which the infidels illegally control, unfolds in accordance with the divine will.

For example, all conquered territory was taken from its infidel false owners and became state property, *fay*, "administered by Islamic law for the benefit of Muslims and their descendants" (Ye'or 2002: 59). Ibn Taymiya (theologian and jurisconsult of the Hanbali school, thirteenth to fourteenth centuries; quoted in Ye'or 2002: 59) explains:

These possessions received the name of *fay* since Allah had taken them away from the infidels in order to *restore* (*afa'a*, *radda*) them to the Muslims. In principle, Allah has created the things of this world only in order that they may contribute to serving him, since he created man only in order to be ministered to. Consequently, the infidels forfeit their persons [in death, slavery, or dimmitude] and their belongings which they do not use in Allah's service to the faithful believers who serve Allah and unto whom Allah restitutes what is theirs; thus is restored to a man the inheritance of which he was deprived, even if he had never before gained possession of it.

Infidels thus have no right to property, even what they have built, grown, or made. All material of value in the world was given by Allah for the benefit of the Muslim community, the *umma*, who are simply fulfilling their duty in reclaiming it from infidel holders.

ALL CHILDREN ARE BORN MUSLIM

"Islamic dogma teaches that all children are born Muslim," (Ye'or 2002: 64) and thus only become Christian, Jewish, Hindu, or pagans through the corrupt imposition of false beliefs. Muslims can look upon this corruption with only pity and disgust. It is understandable that efforts should be made to save the children who were intended by Allah for the *umma*. In Yemen, for example, under a law renewed as recently as 1925, Jewish orphans were taken so that they could "revert" to Islam. Elsewhere throughout the Muslim world, children were commonly or sporadically abducted and converted to Islam:

> The conversion of children to Islam was based on numerous *hadiths* asserting that every child was born a Muslim, based on Koran 30:29–30. . . . The removal of these children from their families thus "restored" children to the *umma*. (Ye'or 2002: 88)

THE DUTY TO HUMILIATE INFIDELS

Bat Ye'or's main subject is the *dhimmi*, those Christians and Jews who accept Islamic dominance, recognize the perfection of the *umma*, and pay *kharaj/jizya* tax for their lives to be spared. Of the many aspects of their lives and histories she discusses, I will mention only one here: "the compulsory degradation of the *dhimmi*." Ye'or (2002: 81) provides an overview:

> To the [Muslim] believer, humiliating the [Christian and Jewish] *dhimmi* constitutes a good deed, an act of faith, and a religious duty, kept constantly alive in the *umma*'s consciousness by a series of ordinances meticulously governing, down to the smallest detail, the organization of degradation that is sacralized into an ethical code.

Ye'or (2002: 81) quotes an ordinance of the caliph al-Amir bi-Ahkam Illah (twelfth century): "Now, the prior degradation of the infidels in this world before the afterlife—where it is their fate [to be degraded]—is considered an act of piety."

A *fatwa* by the Maliki Sheikh al-Adawi (eighteenth century), quoted by Ye'or (2002: 84), states:

> Now there is no doubt that one of the principal conditions of equity consists in banishing infidels from any distinction and any possibility of raising their status, and of reducing them to humiliation and abasement.

There are many means at hand to humiliate and degrade Christian and Jewish *dhimmi*, cataloged in detail by Ye'or. For example, *dhimmi* cannot defend themselves by word or force against any act by a Muslim, or they would be subject to immediate execution; cannot testify in court; cannot ride horses or camels; cannot build houses of worship; cannot ride on a donkey past a Muslim, but have to dismount; cannot raise their voices in the presence of a Muslim; cannot walk to the right of a Muslim, but have to walk to the left; and cannot wear prestigious clothes. When paying their *dhimmi* tax, which they must do in person, they are, by law, slapped. Ye'or (2002: 89) concludes that

> the corpus of his legal disabilities imprisoned the *dhimmi* in that state of ignominy and degradation which provided irrefutable proof of the triumph of Islam. Its superiority is inherent in the relationship between its strength and the humiliation forcibly imposed on others. This opinion, constantly stated in legal and religious texts, expresses a fundamental doctrinal element of government and foreign policy.

ADAM AND EVE WERE MUSLIMS

Having appropriated all the world, all of its wealth, and all of its newborns, Islamic theology then turned to appropriating the past. Far from accepting that Islam was an historical phenomenon that followed Judaism and Christianity and drew on them for inspiration, Islam is projected back in time to the origin of humanity, defining Judaism and Christianity as minor, corrupt offshoots of Islam. Abul Ala Mawdudi (in *Islam: An Historical Perspective*, London: Islamic Foundation, 1980; quoted in Ye'or 2002: 308–309) explains:

> The day Adam and Eve were sent down to live on earth, Allah told them that they were His servants and he was their Master and Creator. . . . This was the simple beginning of Islam. Adam and Eve invited their children to follow the Islamic way of life. They and their children and their later generations followed the teachings of Islam as propounded by Prophet Adam (peace be upon him) for quite a long period.

Later prophets were sent by Allah to teach Islam:

> In short, they were asked to perform a mission—to make
> people righteous and true Muslims. . . . All of them preached
> the same religion—Islam. To mention a few names—Noah,
> Abraham, Moses, Jesus. . . . The people who followed the
> Prophets became Muslims.

In 1999, Sheikh Kamal Khatib (vice-chairman of the Islamic
Movement of Israel, quoted in Ye'or 2002: 310), asserted that
"for us Islam is not only the religion of the Prophet
Muhammad, but also the religion of Moses, Jesus and
Abraham."

From this "historical negationism," as Ye'or calls it, it is but
a small step to asserting Arab presence beyond Arabia prior to
the time of Muhammad. As Yasser Arafat said to the UN in
1974 (quoted in Ye'or 2002: 317):

> The world must know that Palestine was the cradle of the
> most ancient cultures and civilization. Its *Arab people* were
> engaged in farming and building, spreading culture
> throughout the land for thousands of years, setting an
> example in the practice of [religious tolerance and] freedom
> of worship, acting as faithful guardians of the holy places of
> all religions. [Emphasis added.]

THE MYTH OF ISLAMIC TOLERANCE

The idea of Islamic tolerance is not much supported by the
doctrinal or historical evidence. But as with many falsehoods,
there is a grain of truth. Muslims did "tolerate," an apt term,
the existence of Christians and Jews, but only under the stringent conditions of extreme subordination, degradation, and
humiliation, deviations from which were answered by severe

and unrelenting punishment, and often immediate death. Muslims tolerated the *dhimmi*, ironically called "the protected," as the slave owner tolerated his slaves; indeed, *dhimmi* were often reduced to the state of slavery, and those who were not slaves to individual Muslims were slaves to the Muslim *umma* as a whole. As Bernard Lewis (1968, cited in Littman and Ye'or 2005: 95) says:

> The golden age of equal rights [under Islam] was a myth, and belief in it was a result, more than a cause, of Jewish sympathy for Islam. The myth was invented in 19th-century Europe as a reproach to Christians—and taken up by Muslims in our own time as a reproach to Jews. . . . European travellers to the East in the age of liberalism and emancipation are almost unanimous in deploring the degraded and precarious position of Jews in Muslim countries, and the dangers and humiliations to which they were subject. . . . Vambéry [1904] is unambiguous: "I do not know any more miserable, helpless, and pitiful individuals on God's earth than the Jahudi in those countries."

The historical evidence for the degradation of Christian and Jewish *dhimmi* in Muslim lands is overwhelming, both in the sense that it is huge in quantity and virtually unanimous in tone and substance, and in the sense that it is harrowing and profoundly distressing. Much is documented in Bat Ye'or's magisterial *Islam and Dhimmitude: Where Civilizations Collide* (2002). Here I shall present only a few illustrations. Let us begin with Al-Andalus, Islamic Spain, much lauded as an example of a place of Islamic tolerance during a golden age of civilization:

> In a bitter anti-Jewish ode against Joseph Ibn Nagrella (the Jewish minister of the Muslim ruler of Grenada in Spain), Abu Ishaq, a well-known eleventh-century Arab jurist and

poet, is unambiguous: "Put them back where they belong and reduce them to the lowest of the low. . . . Turn your eyes to other [Muslim] countries and you will find the Jews there are outcast dogs. . . . Do not consider it a breach of faith to kill them. . . . They have violated our covenant with them so how can you be held guilty against the violators?"

Of course unpleasant opinions about government ministers are not unknown in even the most civilized countries. What is notable is what happened next: "Nagrella and an estimated five thousand Jews of Grenada were subsequently slaughtered on December 30, 1066" (Littman and Ye'or 2005: 93). This was an impressive event, besting even the most successful eastern European pogroms.

The sentiments expressed by Abu Ishaq in the eleventh century were not so much tied to the period, but rather reflected basic Koranic doctrine, thus making it as apt today as it was a millennium ago. This is clear from Littman and Ye'or:

[Egyptian] President Anwar el-Sadat's declaration on the feast of Muhammad's birth (April 25, 1972). . . . "They [the Jews] shall return and be as the Koran said of them: 'condemned to humiliation and misery.' . . . We shall send them back to their former status." (2005: 93)

And what exactly was their former status? According to Antoine Fattal (1895, quoted in Littman and Ye'or 2005: 94):

The dhimmi is a second-class citizen. If he is tolerated, it is for reasons of a spiritual nature, since there is always the hope that he might be converted; or of a material nature, since he bears almost the whole tax burden. He has his place in society, but he is constantly reminded of his inferiority. . . . In no way is the dhimmi the equal of the Muslim. He is marked out for social inequality and belongs to a despised caste; unequal in regard to individual rights; unequal as regards taxes; unequal in the law courts, as his evidence is not admitted by any Muslim tribunal, and for the same crime his punishment is greater than that imposed on Muslims. No social relationship, no fellowship is possible between Muslims and dhimmis. . . . Even today, the study of the jihad is part of the curriculum of all the Islamic institutes. In the universities of al-Azhar, Najaf, and Zaitouné, students are still taught that the holy war is a binding prescriptive decree, pronounced against the infidels, which will only be revoked with the end of the world.

The Spaniard Badia y Leblich traveled in Morocco at the end of the nineteenth century as a Muslim named Ali Bey, reporting the following in his *Travels of Ali Bey in Morocco* (1899, quoted in Littman and Ye'or 2005):

The Jews of Morocco are in the most abject state of slavery. . . . The Jews are obliged, by order of the Government, to wear a particular dress. . . . When a Jew passes before a mosque, he is obliged to take off his slippers, or sandals; he must do the same when he passes before the house of the Kaid, the Kadi, or of any Mussulman of distinction. At Fez and in some other towns they are obliged to walk barefoot. . . . On my arrival, I had two Jews as my servants; when I saw that they were so ill-treated and vexed in different ways, I asked them why they did not go to another country; they answered me that they could not do so because they were slaves to the sultan.

Circumstances were not happier for Jews in Algeria. William Shaler, the American consul in Algiers from 1816 to 1828, provided the following account (1826, quoted in Littman and Ye'or 2005: 101):

Independent of the legal disabilities of the Jews, they are in
Algiers a most oppressed people; they are not permitted to
resist any personal violence of whatever nature, from a Mussulman; they are compelled to wear clothing of a black or
dark colour; they cannot ride on horseback, or wear arms of
any sort, not even a cane; they are permitted only on Satur-
days and Wednesdays to pass out of the gates of the city
without permission; and on any unexpected call for hard
labour, the Jews are turned out to execute it. . . .

On several occasions of sedition amongst the janissaries,
the Jews have been indiscriminately plundered, and they live
in the perpetual fear of a renewal of such scenes; they are
pelted in the streets even by children, and in short, the whole
course of their existence here, is a state of the most abject
oppression and contumely. The children of Jacob bear these
indignities with wonderful patience; they learn submission
from infancy, and practise it throughout their lives, without
ever daring to murmur at their hard lot. . . . It appears to me
that the Jews at this day in Algiers constitute one of the least
fortunate remnants of Israel existing.

The Chevalier de Hesse-Wartegg reported on the Jews of Tunis
of 1870 (1882, quoted in Littman and Ye'or 2005: 102):

They were neither allowed to ride on horseback nor on a
mule, and even to ride on a donkey was forbidden them
except outside the town; they had then to dismount at the
gates, and walk in the middle of the streets, so as not to be
in the way of Arabs. If they had to pass the "Kasba," they had
first to fall on their knees as a sign of submission, and then
to walk on with lowered head; before coming to a mosque
they were obliged to take the slippers off their feet, and had
to pass the holy edifice without looking at it. As Tunis pos-
sesses no less than five hundred mosques, it will be seen that
Jews did not wear out many shoes at that time. It was worse
even in their intercourse with Musulmans; if one of these

fancied himself insulted by a Jew, he stabbed him at once, and had only to pay a fine to the State, by way of punishment. As late as 1868 seventeen Jews were murdered in Tunis without the offenders having been punished for it: often a Minister or General was in on the plot, to enrich himself with the money of the murdered ones. Nor was that all. The Jews—probably to show their gratefulness for being allowed to live in the town, or to live at all—had to pay 50,000 piastres monthly to the State as a tax.

Paolo della Cella, physician to the ruler of Tripoli, provided the following account of the Jews of Benghazi on the coast of Cyrenaica, Libya, from his trip in 1817 (1822, quoted in Littman and Ye'or 2005: 102):

> The Jews form the labouring portion of the population of Bengasi, the remainder [Muslims] living in idleness at the expense of those unbelievers; in return for which, there is no species of vexation and extortion to which the Israelites are not exposed. They are not permitted to have a dwelling to themselves, but are forced to pay largely for being tolerated in the house of a Mahometan, who thinks he has a right to practise every kind of knavery upon his inmate.

Finally, Edward Lane reports in his acclaimed work *Modern Egyptians*, based on his observations from 1825 to 1835 (1836, quoted in Littman and Ye'or 2005: 103):

> The Jews . . . are held in the utmost contempt and abhorrence by the Muslims in general . . . far more than are the Christians. Not long ago, they used often to be jostled in the streets of Cairo, and sometimes beaten for merely passing on the right hand of a Muslim. At present they are less oppressed; but still they scarcely ever dare to utter a word of abuse when reviled or beaten unjustly by the meanest Arab

or Turk; for many a Jew has been put to death upon false and
malicious accusation of uttering disrespectful words against
the Kuran or the Prophet.

The few observations given here represent a vast literature of
accounts from other outside observers and from participants
themselves, from Al-Andalus to India, of the deprivations suffered by *dhimmi*, both Christian and Jewish, in Muslim lands.
We say nothing about the almost unimaginable experiences of
infidels—Bahais, Hindus, and worshipers of local gods—des-
tined under Islam for conversion, slavery, or the sword.
Reviewing these testimonies, we must conclude that there is
nothing in the historical evidence to support the myth of a
golden age of tolerance under Islam.

PROSPECTS FOR PEACE

Although Arab nationalism and Arab socialism were important ideological mobilizers in the Arab Middle East during the
twentieth century, it would be difficult to imagine that thirteen
centuries of Islamic dogma and practice did not continue to
inform and shape the new strains of thought. In any case, in
recent years there has been an explicit return to Islam as the
dominant ideological mobilizer in the Arab Middle East (and
of course beyond as well, especially in Iran and Pakistan). So
the Muslim theological formulations are obviously relevant to
the course of public affairs in the Middle East.

No less a figure than President George W. Bush has
affirmed his belief that Islam is a religion of peace. Many
who present themselves as learned representatives of Islam
make the same assertion. And most non-Muslims nourish
hopes that this is true. Yet there are disquieting signs in the
Muslim world and on its borders that there is at least a strain

in Islam conducive to belligerent confrontation and aggressive militancy. Bat Ye'or suggests that this strain is well supported by the foundational theology of Islam. To the extent that she is correct, prospects for peace would appear to be increasingly dim.

For example, it is not unusual for the Israeli-Palestinian conflict to be framed as a dispute over land. This might lead one to believe that a pragmatic strategy would likely lead to resolution: confidence-building measures could be followed by compromises about boundaries, with the final result of a peace agreement. If the problem is not a dispute over land, but a confrontation in which the Muslim side believes Allah has ordained that Islam rule and that it is the duty of every Muslim to enforce that principle, then a secular pragmatic solution might have no appeal.

BALANCED OPPOSITION VS. A UNIVERSALISTIC CONSTITUTION OF RULES

From a political point of view, Islam raised tribal society to a higher, more inclusive level of integration. But it was not able to replace the central principle of tribal political organization, balanced opposition, which was honored in the framing of the Muslim vs. infidel opposition. Thus, as with tribal lineage organization, affiliation and loyalty is defined by opposition, and, notwithstanding the common requirements of Islam, the ultimate importance of group membership is not superseded by a universalistic constitution of rules.

The basic tribal framework of "us vs. them" remains, and, in Islam, is validated by God. In the tribal framework, the conception "my group, right or wrong" does not exist, because the question of whether "my group" is right or wrong does not come up. Allegiance is to "my group," period, full stop. Most important, "my group" is defined by and always stands against "the other." An overarching, universalistic, inclusive constitution is not possible. Islam is not a constant referent, but rather, like every level of tribal political organization, is contingent. That is, people act politically as Muslims only when in opposition to infidels. Among Muslims, people will mobilize on a sectarian basis, as Sunni vs. Shi'a. Among Sunni, people will mobilize as the Karim tribe vs. the Mahmud tribe; within the Karim tribe, people will mobilize according to whom they find themselves in opposition to: tribal section vs. tribal section, major lineage vs. major lineage, and so on.

The structural fissiparousness of the tribal order makes very difficult societal cohesion in the Middle East. The particularism of affiliation constantly places people and groups in opposition to one another. There is no universal referent that can include all parties. Oppositionalism is the cultural imperative. Thus the ingenious tribal system, based on balanced opposition, so effectual in supporting decentralized nomads, tends to inhibit societal integration at a more inclusive level, and to preclude civil peace, based on settlement of disputes through legal judgment, at the local level. As is often the case, a structure suitable for one way of life is not readily adaptable to another.

ARAB ATTITUDES TOWARD ISRAEL

We could hardly find a more polarized debate than that about Israel. Even the questions of who Israel's opponents are is a matter of debate: pro-Israel commentators see an Arab war to destroy Israel; pro-Arab commentators define the conflict as between Israel and the usurped Palestinians; Islamic activists think of Israel as a violation of *dar al-Islam*. Almost every important "fact" is contested: who lived in the "Holy Land" and when; who has a legitimate historical claim; how many of this group or that lived there; why some people left; what are the intentions of the contending sides; who is tolerant and inclusive and who is intolerant and exclusive; and so on. Vast literatures exist debating the history, demography, politics, and ethics of this conflict. It is not the intention of this work to rehearse all of these arguments and debates. I shall not attempt to refute analyses different from and contradictory to mine. My purpose in raising this question is to consider the Arab position in terms of our understanding of Arab culture, as set out so far. The discussion, while limited, would not be equally congenial to all interested parties.

If one could look at the Arab–Israeli conflict without prior knowledge, the unrelenting rejection by Arabs of Israel would be difficult to understand. One might imagine that the Arabs, who currently struggle to get along, would look with more enthusiasm to neighbors who could and would assist them in bettering their circumstances, who could help them overcome some of the difficulties that Arabs currently face:

- Most live under a greater or lesser degree of tyranny.
- Many have recently suffered repeated warfare. And in warfare with non-Arabs they have been decisively bested repeatedly.
- Their standard of living—never in modern times outstanding—has plummeted in the last decades, even while many other countries, once at the same level, have shot ahead.
- Their science, long ago an important contribution to world culture, is virtually nonexistent.
- Arab culture, once the glory of civilization, appears to be a shadow of its former self.
- And in consequence of these conditions, Arab influence in the world—except in the sphere of religion—is minor.
- In sum, once important and influential in all spheres of

life, Arab society and culture, aside from religion (about which, more later), have declined in importance and influence. Another way to say this—and perhaps how it feels to Arabs themselves—is that in the global competition with other societies and cultures, Arabs have been losers for centuries.

Once again, on the face of it, one would think, what good fortune for the Arabs to have Israel as a neighbor. Israel could serve both as a model to emulate and a source of practical assistance:

- Israel is a parliamentary democracy with established civil liberties.
- Israeli society is one of the most multiracial and multicultural in the world, as it has gathered Jews from all corners of the world. As well, Israel has accepted and incorporated (if imperfectly) a substantial Arab (Bedouin and Palestinian) population, both Muslim and Christian.
- Israelis—does anyone remember the old compliment?—made the desert bloom. Israeli know-how could help make deserts bloom throughout the Middle East.
- Israeli science and technology is a wonder, with major contributions across the board, including medicine and high technology. This has been recognized by international corporations: IBM and Intel each have three research and development centers in Israel, while Microsoft and Cisco Systems have built their only non-American facilities there. Motorola has its largest research and development site in Israel (David 2005). Two Israelis won the 2005 Nobel Prize for Chemistry.
- Israeli education is first rate, both drawing upon and supporting its scientific and technological establishments. Israel ranks twelfth out of the thirty-five countries

with the world's top five hundred universities (Al-Halyan 2004).

- Israeli industry is innovative and economically successful.
- Furthermore, Israel is a close cousin of the Arabs: Linguistically, Hebrew-speakers are fellow Semites with Arabs; religiously, Jews are "people of the book," recognized and in principle protected by Arabs.

Israel has shown in Africa and elsewhere its willingness to contribute to the development of other societies. Would it not be delighted to contribute to its Arab neighbors?

But in spite of what first impressions, and perhaps sweet reason might suggest, Israel's Arab neighbors have not welcomed it with open arms. On the contrary, the Arabs have rejected not only example and assistance from Israel, but the very existence of Israel. There is not much in human affairs that is absolute, but the Arab rejection of Israel is as close to absolute as possible. The modern founding of Israel is referred to among Arabs as "the catastrophe." What a remarkable reaction to the presence of such a promising potential helpmate. How can we understand and account for this extremist Arab response? It is to this question that we now address ourselves.

I would identify four contributing factors to Arab rejectionism. These are (1) conflicting material interests, (2) use of Israel as an external enemy by Arab leaders to diffuse internal discontent, (3) Arab organizational principles based on opposition, and (4) the challenged honor of the Arabs. These four factors encourage Arab rejection of Israel, and so the rejectionist response is overdetermined, that is, a result of several influences all pushing in the same direction.

The third and fourth factors, the most important, derive from traditional Arab tribal culture and have been incorporated as general principles in Arab cultures.

Conflicting Material Interests

The first factor is conflicting material interests. Much has been made of conflicting Arab and Israeli claims to land and water. Of course, wherever people live together, there are conflicting interests and claims. The question is on what grounds can these conflicts be decided in a mutually acceptable fashion. But note that in this material conflict, the Arab-Israeli opposition is taken as given, while it is what we are trying to explain. So I would suggest that the main problem is the categorical opposition, not the need to share resources and compromise over jurisdictions. Therefore, to my mind this factor is, while not insignificant, the least determining of Arab rejectionism.

Diversion of Internal Discontent

The second factor is the diversion of internal discontent outward toward Israel by Arab rulers. It is the oldest trick in the world to enhance internal solidarity, and thus prop up the position of the rulers, by identifying a threatening external enemy. When piles of oil money and the magic of the mass media are stirred in, the transference strategy becomes even more effective. This factor has been much commented on, and is undoubtedly an important contributor to rejectionism. Israel, close by, small, and initially at least, apparently weak, has proven to be an excellent scapegoat. Once it was clear that Israel was strong, and could really be a threat—General Sharon marching on Cairo!— it became an even better bogeyman. Could Arab rulers survive without Israel to distract "the Arab street"?

Balanced Opposition

The third factor contributing to rejectionism is complementary solidarity or balanced opposition, which is the unity of the closer against the more distant—whether in descent, culture, or religion. As the Arab saying puts it: I against my brother; I and my brother against my cousin; I and my brother and my cousin against the world. The tribal system depended upon this principle—unite with those closer to oppose those more distant—to maintain the balance in complementary opposition. The Italians who returned to Cyrenaica (eastern Libya) in 1911 and fought two wars there during the succeeding decades had expected the Bedouin to turn on their Ottoman overlords and side with them, or at least stay neutral. They learned to their regret that no amount of bribery, cajoling, or stroking, or for that matter threats, could bring the Bedouin onside or keep them neutral. The way the Bedouin saw it (as reported in Evans-Pritchard 1949: 103), their tribes were opposed to one another (and they fought constantly), but the Bedouin were one in the face of the town-dwellers, and the Bedouin and the town-dwellers were one, as Arabs, facing the Turks, and the Arabs and the Turks were one, as Muslims, facing the Christian Italians.

In the conflict with Israel, as always, the most basic Arab social principle is solidarity with the closer in opposition to the more distant. This means that "right" and "wrong" are correlated with "my group" (always right) and "the other group" (always wrong). The morality is that one must strive always to advantage one's own group and to disadvantage the other group. Unity, then, is possible only in opposition to those more distant. And to those more distant, only ill will.

For Arab Muslims confronting Jews, the opposition is between the *dar al-Islam*, the land of Islam and peace, and the *dar al-harb*, the land of the infidels and conflict. The Muslim is obliged to advance God's true way, Islam, in the face of the ignominy of the Jew's false religion. Islamic doctrine holds that all non-Muslims, whether Christian or Jewish *dhimmi* or infidel pagans, must be subordinate to Muslims. Jews, under

Koranic doctrine, are inherently inferior by virtue of their false religion, and must not be allowed to be equal to Muslims. For Muslim Arabs, the conceit of Jews establishing their own state, Israel, and on territory conquered by Muslims and since Muhammad under the control of Muslims, can only be considered outrageous and intolerable.

We must ask ourselves, can these traditional oppositions remain central to the Arabs and the Middle East? Has not modernization, urbanization, and education shaken the hold of the old oppositional models? As Ajami (1999: 155) puts it, "Underneath the modern cover there remained the older realities of sects, ethnicity, and the call of the clans." The poet Khalil Hawi wrote in 1980 (quoted in Ajami 1999: 92) that the modernist "Arab awakening" had been a pretense that had "covered up the total backwardness of Arab society." Ajami (1999: 92) continues: "In the 'modern' political movements littering the landscape, he saw nothing but the hold of old 'tribal, sectarian, and clannish loyalties.'"

There is no way, in this structure, to reach beyond the Arab vs. Israeli and Muslim vs. Jew opposition to establish a currently unthinkable common interest, short of an unimagined attack on both Arabs and Israelis by some group deemed by both more distant (religiously, racially, culturally). In this oppositional framework, it is impossible and inappropriate to seek or see common interests or common possibilities. Israel will always be the distant "other" to be disadvantaged and, if possible, conquered.

Honor

The fourth factor in rejectionism is Arab honor. As documented above, Arab honor consists in the warrior's imperative to stand up for oneself and one's people against outsiders, and in success in confrontations with outsiders. But only the victorious have

honor, and the more the defeated are crushed, the greater the
honor to the victors. As Ajami (1999: 134) says, in the Arab
"world . . . triumph rarely comes with mercy or moderation."

We can understand Arab honor if we consider the importance of tribal organization in Arab culture. To summarize
what we have already established, tribal organization requires
the balance of segments (i.e., lineages of kinsmen) against one
another. Peace and security, to the extent that it can exist,
resides in the balance of segments, which serves to deter
aggressive adventures by promising swift retaliation. But this
balance only works as deterrence if people are willing to stand
up and defend themselves and their group. The concept of
honor is the cultural demand that each person must stand up
and do his or her duty. One keeps one's honor by doing one's
segmentary duty. Arabs are taught, and many have taken to
heart, that honor is more important than anything—than
wealth, than fame, than love, than death.

Deeply imbued with the value of honor, today's Arab finds
himself in a virtually untenable situation. Looking back to the
years of glory under Muhammad, when the Bedouin armies
imposed Islam by the sword in the Middle East outside Arabia,
in North Africa, Persia, India, central Asia, and much of
southern Europe—the baseline reference point for Arab culture—and the later defeat of the Crusaders, Arabs can only
view subsequent history as a sad tale of defeat visited upon
defeat. First there was the breakdown of Arab solidarity and
fighting among the Arabs themselves. Then the Arabs were
conquered and governed by the Turkish Ottoman Empire. The
decline and fall of the Ottomans led to conquest and occupation of almost all of the Arab lands by the despised Christians
of Europe. So during the last two centuries, the Arabs lost time
after time, and lived under the rule of infidels. Even their successful anticolonial struggles turned into empty victories, or
worse than empty, for the Arab victors found themselves sub-

ject to their own power-hungry statists, sadistic despots, or religious fanatics.

What honor can be found in defeat and oppression? And what self-respect can Arabs find without honor? In a world of defeat and failure, honor can be found only in resistance. Facing their many weaknesses and the great strengths of their adversaries, Arab self-respect demands honor be vindicated through standing and fighting, no matter what the cost. Where there is honor, no victory, or even loss, can be Pyrrhic, for no cost, even life, can be too great.

Osama bin Ladin on one of his publicized tapes complained bitterly the loss of Andalusia, retaken from the Arabs by Spain in the fifteenth century! Imagine the chagrin and shame that Jews—who for a thousand years and more had been *dhimmi*, "protected" subordinates of the Arabs—had established themselves in the Arab heartland (never mind that the Jews had been there first) as an independent state and had repeatedly fought and beaten all of the Arab armies. Disaster! Catastrophe! Where is Arab honor? Are there among the Arabs no men? As *Al Jazeera* editor in chief Ahmed Sheikh said in a recent interview (Heumann 2006):

> Heumann: Who is responsible for the [lack of democracy in the Middle East]?
>
> Sheikh: The Israeli-Palestinian conflict is one of the most important reasons why these crises and problems continue to simmer. The day when Israel was founded created the basis for our problems. . . .
>
> Heumann: Do you mean to say that if Israel did not exist, there would suddenly be democracy in Egypt, that the schools in Morocco would be better, that the public clinics in Jordan would function better?
>
> Sheikh: I think so.
>
> Heumann: Can you please explain to me what the Israeli-Palestinian conflict has to do with these problems?

Sheikh: The Palestinian cause is central for Arab thinking.
Heumann: In the end, is it a matter of feelings of self-esteem?
Sheikh: Exactly. It's because we always lose to Israel. It gnaws at the people in the Middle East that such a small country as Israel, with only about 7 million inhabitants, can defeat the Arab nation with its 350 million. That hurts our collective ego. The Palestinian problem is in the genes of every Arab.

Of course, editor in chief Sheikh does not, talking to a Western audience, speak of losing to the despised Jews, or use such indigenous terms as "honor." But it is clear from his explanation that it is the loss of honor that "hurts our collective ego."

A more eloquent cry of despair forced itself from the heart of the Lebanese poet Khalil Hawi. Fouad Ajami (1999: 26) begins his lengthy and profound, sensitive and beautiful essay "The Suicide of Khalil Hawi: Requiem for a Generation," with a few of the simple facts:

Khalil Hawi, a poet of renown and professor at the American University of Beirut (the AUB), educated at that university and at Cambridge, killed himself in the late evening on June 6, 1982, at the age of sixty-two, on the balcony of his home in West Beirut. A troubled and sensitive man of great literary talent, he had picked a dramatic occasion for his death: Earlier in the day, in midmorning, Israeli armor had struck into Lebanon. Israel had come to put an end to the Palestinian sanctuary in Lebanon, to be rid of the running war on its northern border with the forces of the Palestine Liberation Organization, which it had fought over the preceding decade. "Where are the Arabs?" Hawi had asked his colleagues on the university campus before he went home and shot himself. "Who shall remove the stain of shame from my forehead?"

Hawi's sentiments were, not surprisingly, well represented in his poetry. As Ajami (1999: 97) referring to Hawi's 1979 volume, *Wounded Thunder*, puts it, "He wept for himself and for that 'Arab nation' whose salvation he had so much wanted to see:

> How heavy is the shame,
> do I bear it alone?
> Am I the only one to cover my face with ashes?
> The funerals that the morning announces
> echo in the funeral at dusk.
> There is nothing over the horizon,
> save for the smoke of black embers."

If military defeat was not sufficient humiliation, Arabs had only to compare their failed societies with prosperous, dynamic, developed Israel. In these circumstances, the only way to salvage Arab honor was to reject, forever, the Jewish intrusion. To accept Israel—"the Zionist entity"—is to admit defeat to the lowest of enemies. Nothing, then, would be left of Arab honor. Rejectionism, to the Arab mind, is the only honorable path.

These four factors—the defense of honor, segmentary opposition, transference of discontent outward, and conflicting material interests—militate in favor of alienation between the Arabs and Israel and the tenacious rejectionism of the Arabs. The two cultural factors—honor and opposition—are influences deeply embedded in Arab character. What appears to be reasonable to Westerners will not appear reasonable to Arabs. Such is the power of culture.

The Return to Religion

But another question remains. Why is Arab rejectionism increasingly expressed in religious terms? I saw a similar turn toward religion during my research in Baluchistan in southeastern Iran (Salzman 2000: ch. 12). The Baluch had been conquered by Reza Shah in the 1930s and been ruled by Iran since then. The Baluch, at one time proud warriors and raiders, were forced to accept that they were inferior in power, wealth, and technology to the Persians. But almost all of the Baluch were Sunni, and the Persians Shi'a, so the Baluch could at least claim superiority in religion. Some even said that the Shi'a Persians were not really Muslims. Whatever the evidence of success or failure in this world, however one does in the competition for power, wealth, and prestige, one can always claim that one's religion is superior, and, even better, that your opponents are agents of the forces of darkness.

In worldly terms, in military, economic, technological, and scientific power, Israel since its founding has gone from strength to strength, while the Arabs have gone from defeat to defeat and failure to failure. Righting this humiliation has proven extremely difficult. But the turn to religion allows the Arabs to claim that Islam is the true faith and Jews are evil infidels. Thus Muslim Arabs will always be right and Israeli Jews wrong. And, in this perspective, rewards for virtue, which for Arabs are so rare in this world, can be sought in the hereafter. In this usage, religion is the last refuge of the worldly failure.

An appreciation of the multiple and profound factors underlying the Arab rejection of Israel belies simple analyses, judgments, and solutions of the Arab-Israeli conflict. Any solution would have to be grounded not just in practical proposals and compromises, but in new attitudes and new perspectives, which are much more difficult.

"ISLAM'S BLOODY BORDERS"

The conflict between Arabs and Israelis, Muslims and Jews is not the only major conflict between Muslims and others. On the contrary, military contestations on the borders of lands dominated by Muslims are pervasive. In a controversial article, and then in his book, Samuel Huntington (1996: 254–58) argues that conflicts are particularly prevalent between Muslims and non-Muslims.

> The overwhelming majority of fault line conflicts, . . . have taken place along the boundary looping across Eurasia and Africa that separates Muslims from non-Muslims. While at the macro or global level of world politics the primary clash of civilizations is between the West and the rest, at the micro or local level it is between Islam and the others.
>
> Intense antagonisms and violent conflicts are pervasive between local Muslim and non-Muslim peoples.

Bosnians vs. Serbs, Turks vs. Greeks, Turks vs. Armenians, Azeris vs. Armenians, Tatars vs. Russians, Afghans and Tajiks vs. Russians, Uighurs vs. Han Chinese, Pakistanis vs. Indians, Sudanese Arabs vs. southern Sudanese Christians and animists, northern Nigerians vs. southern, among others, are ongoing conflicts between Muslims and others. As Huntington (1996: 256) puts it:

> Wherever one looks along the perimeter of Islam, Muslims have problems living peaceably with their neighbors. . . . Muslims make up about one-fifth of the world's population but in the 1990s they have been far more involved in intergroup violence than the people of any other civilization. The evidence is overwhelming.
>
> There were, in short, three times as many intercivilizational conflicts involving Muslims as there were conflicts between all non-Muslim civilizations.

Furthermore, Muslim states were twice as militarized as Christian countries (Huntington 1996: 258). And finally, in conflicts, Muslim states were much more violent than others (Huntington 1996: 258):

> Muslim states also have had a high propensity to resort to violence in international crises, employing it to resolve 76 crises out of a total of 142 in which they were involved between 1928 and 1979. . . . When they did use violence, Muslim states used high-intensity violence, resorting to full-scale war in 41 percent of the cases where violence was used and engaging in major clashes in another 39 percent of the cases. While Muslim states resorted to violence in 53.5 percent, violence was used by the United Kingdom in only 11.5 percent, by the United States in 17.9 percent, and by the Soviet Union in 28.5 percent of the crises in which they were involved. . . . Muslim bellicosity and violence are late-twentieth-century facts which neither Muslims nor non-Muslims can deny.

Huntington wrote this before the 9/11 attacks on the United States and the events that have followed. These events would seem to confirm Huntington's analysis.

Chapter 6

TRIBE AND STATE

The Dynamics of Incompatibility

What part can we say that tribal organization and culture plays in contemporary Middle Eastern life? Would we not be justified in saying that tribes in the Middle East are primarily of historical interest, with little influence in modern Middle Eastern societies? After all, in the Middle East there are established state organizations, with governments, bureaucracies, police, courts, armies, political parties, and so on. If Middle Eastern countries are modern countries, with modern institutions, the influence of tribes and tribal life and culture must be minimal or nonexistent. It would then follow that the thesis of this volume, that Middle Eastern culture is imbued with tribal culture and organization, particularly "balanced opposition," and that this underlies many aspects of contemporary Middle Eastern life, must be heavily discounted or rejected altogether.

175

To support the thesis of this volume, that tribal organization and culture remain heavily influential in the Middle East,
would require showing that recent and contemporary Middle
Eastern societies are not "modern" in the sense that Euro-
American societies are, and that the tribal spirit continues to
hold sway in the Middle East. This I shall try to demonstrate
here.

THE PERVASIVENESS OF TRIBES AND TRIBAL CULTURE IN THE MIDDLE EAST

I went to Baluchistan in southeastern Iran for the first time in
1968. This was perhaps the most remote region of Iran, and
admitted by all to be a tribal area. One of the first questions
asked of me by the Baluch was how big my lineage was. As has
been explained in earlier chapters, in tribal politics there is
strength in numbers. Perhaps the assumption of the Baluch
was that, as I had bravely come so far from home to live intrep-
idly amid strangers, and was obviously wealthy, having a new
Land Rover, I must come from a large and powerful lineage.
When I said that we had no lineages, the Baluch were incredu-
lous. What did we do then, they asked, when there was
trouble, when we were threatened, when we needed support?
Why, we went to the police, I said. They laughed; they roared.
Then they looked at me pityingly. Oh, no, no, no, they said;
only your lineage mates will help you.

In fact, states and state institutions have existed in the
Middle East for at least four thousand years. There have been
governments, police, courts, tax collectors, armies, and so on,
far back into the distant past of the Middle East (Kramer 1963;
Oppenheim 1964; Trigger 2003). But they were never really
there to serve people generally. These state institutions were
put into place to serve the people controlling them. Any
moments of disinterested leadership or wise attention to the

needs of the populace were followed by centuries of self-serving seeking, rent collecting, and thuggery. The populace of these states were not made of citizens, but subjects; they did not have needs to be served nor rights to be honored, but duties to perform and resources to be extracted. For their own security and comfort, the populace was left on its own to look after its own interests (Gellner 1988).

Tribal organization served the needs of the populace in several ways. First, a more remote tribe could reject claims of state agents and operate independently by defending itself against state incursions and extractions either militarily or through escaping by moving farther into the hinterland. As we have seen, the Turkmen of northeastern Iran escaped the Persian crown's punitive expeditions in this fashion (Irons 1975). The Yarahmadzai Baluch avoided the military grasp of Reza Shah for years by means of this tactic (Arfa 1964: 253–57; Salzman 2000). Second, strong tribes could themselves attack and capture the state apparatus, which they would then apply for their own benefit, a process so common in Middle Eastern history that it was conceptualized in Ibn Khaldun's model, which applies throughout the Arab world and beyond. As Peter Avery (1965) points out regarding Iranian history:

> Karim Khan [Safavid] reintroduced yet another endemic feature of Iranian political power. His roots were tribal. . . . [This reflected] the 'two nation' character of Iran, as between the nomad and the settled portions of the population. . . .
>
> In the history of Iranian dynasties, his successors, the Qajars, also achieved victory for a tribe. With one of their members making himself Shah of Iran, the Qajar tribe for a time perpetuated tribal hegemony; tribal in origin only, however. In the manner of their rise to power they exploited the tribal strand in the Persian social complex but later the Qajar Shahs gave the tribes short shrift.

Third, tribes could sell their services to the state, thus removing any threat, overt or implied, to the state. For example, the Al Murrah Bedouin of the Empty Quarter received a salary to participate in the National Guard of Saudi Arabia (Cole 1975). Fourth, as described above in detail, tribes could protect their members against depredations by other tribes. Fifth, tribes as regional organizations provided wide geographical range for the extensive adaptation of pastoralism. Sixth, tribes could provide welfare services for their members, such as fostering children, providing livestock or produce in case of need, and contributing collective labor to large projects. I have seen this repeatedly among the Yarahmadzai Baluch (Salzman 2000).

There is a spatial dimension to state-tribe relations, in that states tend to be strongest at their centers and weaker at greater distances, and thus tribes on the peripheries tend to be more independent of the state. But it would be an error—both historically and geographically incorrect—to think of tribes and states as geographically separated. It would be more accurate to think of states and tribes as alternative forms of organization that shared space and power, compromising to a greater or lesser degree, depending upon the circumstances. One point is abundantly clear: the presence of state forms of organization by no means precludes the existence, presence, and influence of tribal forms of organization. We thus find in the Middle East the coexistence—often uneasy—between states and tribes.

There are a variety of strategies to lubricate state-tribe relations. One is by using marriages to establish dynastic alliances through affinal ties and, following offspring, blood ties. For example, Mohammed Reza Shah, king of Iran, married Soraya Isfandiari, daughter of a leading Khan of the Bakhtiari tribe, one of the largest, richest, and most powerful in Iran (Avery 1965: 346, 418). Another is bribery, or, to use a nicer term, patronage, as with the Bedouin tribal populations incorporated into Middle Eastern armies, such as Jordan's and Saudi

Arabia's (Lancaster 1997; Cole 1975). A third is "progressions," Geertz's (1983) term for the regular visits of the head of state and his escort to all regions of the country.

In some Middle Eastern countries, the population is almost entirely tribal or of recent tribal background.

- **Libya** (Evans-Pritchard 1949; Davis 1987), **Saudi Arabia** (Cole 1975; Lancaster 1997), and **Oman** (Chatty 1996; Barth 1983: ch. 5) have always been dominated by tribes, the peasant and urban populations being largely insignificant. During the August 3, 2005, crowning of Saudi Arabia's King Abdullah (*Ottawa Citizen* 2005: A8), "hundreds of tribal chiefs, Islamic clerics, princes and commoners pledged loyalty."

In other Middle Eastern countries, tribes occupy the deserts and mountains, but are also present in the plains and plateaus.

- In **Iran** the peasant villages, towns, and cities of the great central plateau are surrounded by tribes occupying the mountains and deserts (Avery 1965; Fisher 1968). But tribal territory penetrates deep into the plateau as well. Two of the great tribes regularly engage two of the great cities: the Bakhtiari summer in the vicinity of Isfahan (Garthwaite 1983a, 1983b), while the Qashqai summer outside of Shiraz (Beck 1986, 1991).
- In **Kuwait**, a desert country, tribes are a major part of the population. In the recent debate over women's electoral rights, part of the strong opposition arose from "conservative tribal MPs," members of Parliament elected by tribal populations (Haddadin 2005: A10). In municipal council elections of June 2, 2005, "Tribal candidates bagged six of the 10 elected seats, . . . while two were claimed by members backed by Sunni and Shiite

Islamists and two won by Liberal-leaning businessmen" (Hasan 2005). With minority Islamists and modernists split, the majority tribal members dominate.

- In **Iraq** too, much of the population is tribal. It was no accident that Ghazi al-Yawar, the post–Saddam Hussein interim president, and newly elected Iraqi government vice president, is a sheikh of a major tribe, the great Shammar confederacy. Saddam Hussein himself came from the al-Bu Nasir tribe, from which the tribal leader, Sheikh Mahmoud Nidha, ran for Parliament in the 2005 election. Sheika Lamea abed Khaddouri, elected to the new Iraqi Parliament but assassinated in April 2005, was the daughter of a leader of the Rabiya tribe. Even the towns are heavily tribal, and contact with the population is often through tribal leaders.
- **Syria**, **Jordan**, and **Israel** have substantial Bedouin populations (Lancaster and Lancaster 1999; Marx 1967; Kressel 1996, 2003; Meir 1996). In Jordan, the Bedouin are the backbone of the army. Bedouin also play a limited but useful role in the Israeli army.
- **Egypt** is a peasant country par excellence, with the bulk of the population living in the Nile Valley. But the eastern and western deserts are occupied by tribes (Abou-Zeid 1959; Hobbs 1989; Cole and Altorki 1998), and many of the Nile Valley peasants are descended from Bedouin who were on the losing side in tribal wars (Evans-Pritchard 1949).
- In the Maghreb, including **Morocco**, **Algeria**, and **Tunisia**, tribes occupy the mountains and deserts, but are important on the plains as well (Gellner 1969; Gellner and Micaud 1973).

Tribal organization and culture are the warp and weft of Middle Eastern society. This is sometimes hidden by the knotted pile of

peasants and townsmen, merchants and government func-
tionaries, imams and sufis, and villages and cities. But, to
change the metaphor, scratch a townsman or urbanite, and
under the patina a tribesman will often be found.

Events in the Middle East that appear to be geopolitical or
motivated by state politics turn out on examination to have
important tribal components. For example, in Iraq in
2004–2005, we hear of Iraqi insurgents attacking the occupying
Americans, or of Sunni supporters of Saddam Hussein
attacking officials of the newly elected Shi'a-dominated government. It was reported on May 11, 2005, that "Al-Qaeda Captures Iraqi Governor" (*National Post*, A12), which appears to be
international Islamic insurgents attacking the Iraqi government. But a closer inspection shows the tribal matrix within
which this has occurred:

> Governor [of western Iraq's Anbar Province] Nawaf Raja
> Farhan al-Mahalawi . . . was abducted amid a feud between
> his Abu Mahal tribe, which wields influence in the region,
> and insurgents linked to al-Qaeda frontman Abu Musab al-
> Zarqawi. . . .
>
> "Men of the Governor's tribe went against Zarqawi's
> rebels, sparking clashes that lasted a week between the two
> groups," said one of the sources. . . .
>
> Mr. Mahalawi's kidnappers, meanwhile, were demand-
> ing his tribe release some of the Zarqawi followers it is
> holding.

This kidnapping is a consequence of a conflict between local
tribes and foreign fighters arriving in Iraq to fight the new
regime. As Nancy Youssef and Yasser Salihee (2005: A11)
describe it:

> An Iraqi official said the [recent American and Iraqi Govern-
> ment] offensive [around Qaim in northern Ambar Province]

was triggered by tribal leaders' complaints that about 300 foreign fighters had overtaken the town and were attacking residents who didn't offer refuge.

"They said, 'We are citizens of Qaim and we are now being attacked by non-Iraqi people coming from Syria. They are shelling us with mortars'," Bruska Noori Shaways, the deputy Iraqi defence minister, said in an interview.

The well-armed foreign fighters apparently believed that they could dictate terms to the local Iraqi population. They should have realized that the local people were part of a tribal network and could mobilize fighters of their own, and as well had sufficient weight to call upon the government to provide support.

These events indicate the continuing importance of tribes in contemporary Anbar Province and more generally in Iraq (Kaplan 2007). However, Anbar Province includes all of western Iraq and borders on Syria to the north, Jordan to the west, and Saudi Arabia to the south. Anbar Province is "renowned for its deeply rooted conservativism and tribalism" (Abedin 2005: A19).

What can we conclude from the kidnapping? First, we see that the governor becomes governor at least partly because his Abu Mahal tribe is powerful in the region. Second, we see that the Abu Mahal and other tribes do not have a high level of tolerance for outside military forces throwing their weight around in their tribal territory. Third, it is evident that the Abu Mahal tribe is able to mobilize as a military force. Fourth, the Abu Mahal tribe was willing and able to take on al Qaeda forces under al-Zarqawi, and to engage them militarily over time. Finally, Abu Mahal and other tribal leaders have sufficient weight to call upon the government to provide substantial support, in this case a full-scale military campaign with heavy American participation.

There is nothing surprising about the reaction of the Abu

Mahal and other Anbar tribes. They are committed to maintaining their independence and their control over their region. This is conceptualized for the Abu Mahal, and among tribesmen throughout the Middle East, as maintaining their honor. Falling under the domination of others results in the loss of honor. This is deeply encoded in tribal culture. At least some of the resistance to the American forces and their allies is due to the sense of lost honor.

> Said Ahmed Jassim, a religious student in the flashpoint city of Fallujah, as he cheered an attack on a U.S. convoy recently. "We are fighting for our country, for our honour, for Islam. We are not doing this for Saddam."
> "Everyone is with the resistance, said Safa Hamad Hassan, 22, whose cousin was wounded when a tank round landed near his home during the fighting. "Saddam Hussein is finished. We are protecting our honour and our land." (Beeston 2003: A9)

The pervasiveness of concern for honor is a strong indication of the continued power of tribal culture.

STATE-BUILDING IN TRIBAL SOCIETIES

In the light of the nature of tribal organization and culture, and particularly the central principle of balanced opposition, what kind of broader society and state can be built upon this foundation? Tribal life is characterized by one of two situations: either the balance is effective, leading to unending and unlimited factional conflict, or the effective balance breaks down, and one party is able to dominate, which in the tribal context usually means that the weaker parties are driven out altogether. Imagining societies of this spirit, we would find those fractionalized into competing warlords, and those dominated completely by a strong party that does its best to monopolize all power.

The spirit of intertribal politics is "winner take all." As Ben-Meir (2005: 3) puts it, "The common perception in a tribal society [is] . . . that any social contest is a zero-sum game in which the gain of one is considered a loss to the other." In the Middle East, all honor goes to the victor; the vanquished is dishonored. There is no honor in "playing fairly," "doing your best," or "upholding the rules." Winning, to paraphrase a famous American football coach, is not the best thing, it is the only thing. Applied to state governance, this spirit advises monopoly of power, ruthless suppression of opponents, and accumulation of benefits. In short, it is a recipe for despotism, for tyranny.

In the Middle East, both outcomes of the tribal spirit are evident, in many cases alternating as circumstances allow.

- **Iraq** during the second half of the twentieth century was dominated ruthlessly by members of the minority Sunni community, under the Baath national socialist banner. All opposition, no matter how passive, was suppressed with the utmost prejudice. The spoils of the society were accumulated and enjoyed by the rulers and their supporters. With the overthrow of the Baath regime by the invasion of American and allied forces, Iraq has fallen into violent factional conflict consisting of mass murders and large-scale reprisals.
- **Syria** has been thoroughly dominated during the second half of the twentieth century by members of the Alawite minority, also under the Baath national socialist banner. Opposition has been effectively snuffed out. The Islamist movement in Hama was silenced when, infamously, that city was leveled by government artillery, killing tens of

thousands. In the last decade of the twentieth century, Syria extended its domination to **Lebanon**, imposing its interest through its military and secret service, occupying the country and controlling its government.

- In the Hashemite Kingdom of **Jordan**, power remains in the hands of·the hereditary monarchy, which uses its Bedouin-based army to control its Palestinian peasant and urban population.
- **Saudi Arabia** boasts an absolute monarchy, based on an alliance with Wahabi clerics and the support of Bedouin tribal auxiliaries. The large royal family lives in unimaginable luxury.
- **Egypt** is a one-party state governed by presidents-for-life. Opposition, including religious movements, has been brutally suppressed. The government is notoriously corrupt.
- **Libya**, after a military coup that deposed the king, has been governed by Colonel Ghaddafi. Opposition, internal and external, has been eliminated by any and all means (Davis 1987).
- Elections in **Algeria** are honored, unless the government of the day does not like the results. When the Stalinist government was voted out in favor of the religious opposition, the government rejected the result and refused to turn over the levers of power. The religious opposition initiated a guerilla war, annihilating village after village, with the government striking back brutally. The civil war continues. Whoever becomes the ultimate victor, the despotism will continue.
- In **Morocco**, royalty and religious sanction combine in a hereditary dynasty based on a sacred lineage (Combs-Schilling 1989). Opposition is not tolerated.
- Beyond the Arab world, in **Iran**, a theocracy violently replaced the Pahlavi dynasty, which itself had been

established by a military coup. The self-renewing high council of religious figures is the ultimate arbiter of society, the decisions of which override any wishes of the electorate. Therefore, as elected officials must be pre-approved by the council, and are in practice impotent, the elaborate electoral process is a futile sham. Opposition newspapers are closed down, reporters are eliminated, and opposition demonstrations are broken up and participants beaten and imprisoned.

- **Afghanistan**, still much under direct tribal control, throughout the twentieth century repeatedly alternated between fragmentation and balanced opposition between tribal "warlords," on the one hand, and despotic control by powerful central parties, such as the Soviet-supported communist regime, and the Islamist Taliban. The present weak central government is surrounded by powerful tribes in the periphery, particularly the Pakhtun tribes in the south, and current hopes for a stable, democratic regime rest on American and NATO troops.

The despotism of these countries goes beyond total control of political power, beyond the lack of democracy and use of all means to suppress opposition. The tyranny also defines governance, which is seen not as service to the public, but as the capture of public resources for the benefit of the powerful. The kleptocratic spirit characteristic of these countries was illustrated nicely by Saddam Hussein under UN economic boycott by his building yet more luxurious palaces as his subjects suffered without sufficient food or medicine. Government bureaucracies in these countries are not so much facilitators of services as rent-seeking operations demanding a cut of every exchange taking place in the society.

As one would expect in these circumstances, governments lean toward a command or controlled economy, leading to poor

economic performance, and public services are mediocre, ineffec-
tual, or absent entirely. Whatever the virtues of Middle Easterners,
and however rich their cultures, it is difficult to be enthusiastic
about the state of Middle Eastern countries today. Few Middle
Easterners are. The glories of the past are distant memories.

The Critical Arab Voice

Negative assessment of Middle Eastern society and culture has
been dismissed by "postcolonial" theorists such as Edward
Said (1978) and his many fellow travelers as so much malevo-
lent propaganda intended as rationale and camouflage for
Western imperialism and colonialism against the Middle East
and its innocent inhabitants. Cultural analysis of the Middle
East is dismissed by postcolonial thinkers as "reductionist
essentialism" meant to demean rather than illuminate. Westerners and other outsiders are excluded from the right to com-
ment about the Middle East, except perhaps to flatter and provide political support. These attitudes have diffused to the
wider public in the form of multicultural political correctness,
which insists that every culture and every country is equally
good in all respects as every other, except perhaps the decadent
and criminal West, and that never a discouraging word should
be uttered about non-Western cultures and societies. Many
readers would thus be inclined to dismiss out of hand the
remarks critical of the Middle East appearing in this and earlier chapters. For this reason, we now turn to a respected cri-
tique of the Arab Middle East by Arab scholars and researchers.
    Under the auspices of the UN Development Program and
the Arab Fund for Economic and Social Development, an
independent group of Arab authors and advisers prepared the
Arab Human Development Report 2002. The lead author is Nader
Fergany and the core team members are Ali Abdel Gadir Ali,

M. M. Al-Imam, George Corm, Osama El-Kholy, Taher Kanaan, Hoda Rashad, and M. Gawad Reda. The advisory group of twenty Arab scholars was led by Rima Khalaf Hunaidi. The volume begins with the authors establishing their bona fides by blaming Israel for the many flaws and shortcomings to be described (UNDP 2002:1). But most of the volume consists of assessment, drawing on a wide range of studies and databases of the current circumstances in the nineteen Arab countries surveyed, and of recommendations for correcting the many weaknesses. Many of the assessments place the Arab world in a worldwide context.

The Arab world is deemed to suffer from a "freedom deficit" (UNDP 2002: 27), as measured by established indices:

Out of seven world regions, the Arab countries had the lowest freedom score in the late 1990s. . . . The Arab region also has the lowest value [score] of all regions for voice and accountability.

On the freedom index, which focuses on political freedom during 1998–99, the scores were as follows (UNDP 2002: 27, figure 2.4, estimates from a bar graph):

North America	1.00
Oceania	0.95
Europe	0.82
Latin Amer. & Carib.	0.65
South & East Asia	0.40
Sub-Saharan Africa	0.38
Arab countries	0.15

The Arab countries not only rank last, but the gap even between the Arab countries and the next-to-last-ranking Africa is substantial.

The index on "voice and accountability" is based on "a number of indicators measuring various aspects of the political process, civil liberties, political rights, and the independence of the media" (UNDP 2002: 27). The scores (UNDP 2002: 27, figure 2.5, estimates from a bar graph) for 1998 are as follows:

North America	1.50
Oceania	1.30
Europe	0.80
Latin Amer. & Carib.	0.20
South & East Asia	−0.45
Sub-Saharan Africa	−0.60
Arab countries	−0.90

There is a "women's empowerment deficit" (UNDP 2002: 28):

> Applying the UNDP gender empowerment measure (GEM) to Arab countries clearly reveals that the latter suffer a glaring deficit in women's empowerment. Among regions of the world, the Arab region ranks next to last as measured by GEM; only sub-Saharan Africa has a lower score.

The ranking for GEM scores is as follows (UNDP 2002: 28, figure 2.7, estimates from a bar graph):

North America	0.64
Oceania	0.51
Europe	0.49
Latin Amer. & Carib.	0.39
South & East Asia	0.35
Arab countries	0.26
Sub-Saharan Africa	0.24

Education, as a means of developing human capabilities, has not been well developed in the Arab world. "Educational achievement in the Arab countries as a whole, judged even by traditional criteria, is still modest when compared to elsewhere in the world, even in developing countries" (UNDP 2002: 51). Illiteracy in the world for 1995 is indicated as follows (UNDP 2002: 51, figure 4.1, estimates from a bar graph):

Arab countries	43.0%
Developing countries	29.5%
Industrialized countries	2.0%

Gross school enrollment percentage in Arab countries is well below the average of developing countries, not to mention industrialized societies. The percentage of students in higher education in the Arab world is a quarter of the level of the developed countries, a third of that of Asia/Oceania, and well behind Latin America and the Caribbean. The results are the same for women in higher education. Worse, per capita expenditure on education in the Arab world dropped from 20 percent in 1980 to 10 percent in 1995, in relation to expenditure in the industrialized countries.

Arab countries are not moving toward knowledge-based societies, as measured by scientific and technological development (UNDP 2002: 65):

Arab countries have some of the lowest levels of research funding the world. . . . R & D expenditure as a percentage of GDP [gross domestic product] was a mere 0.4 for the Arab world in 1996, compared with 1.26 in 1995 for Cuba, 2.35 in 1994 for Israel and 2.9 for Japan.

Scientific production as measured by scientific papers per unit of population showed equally poor results (UNDP 2002: 66):

The average output of the Arab world per million inhabitants is roughly 2 per cent of that of an industrialized country. . . .

In 1981, China was producing half the output [scientific papers] of the Arab world; by 1987, its output had equalled that of Arab countries; it now produces double their output. In 1981, the Republic of Korea was producing 10 per cent of the output of the Arab world; in 1995, it almost equalled its output.

In frequently cited scientific papers, with more than forty citations, per million inhabitants, Switzerland scored 79.90, the United States 42.99, and Israel 38.63, while the Arab countries trailed badly: Kuwait led the pack with 0.53, followed by Saudi Arabia with 0.07, Egypt 0.02, and Algeria 0.01 (UNDP 2002: 67).

The Arab world, while comparable to other developing regions as regards telephone lines and personal computers, trails all other regions with regard to Web sites and Internet users (UNDP 2002: 74–75).

In exploring "Using human capabilities: recapturing economic growth and reducing human poverty," the picture of the Arab world continues to appear gloomy (UNDP 2002: 85, 87):

GDP in all Arab countries combined stood at $531.2 billion in 1999—less than that of a single European country, Spain ($595.5 billion).

. . . GNP [gross national product] per worker in all Arab countries combined was less than half that of two comparator developing countries: Argentina and the Republic of Korea. (Note: The GNP of the Republic of Korea outstrips that of all Arab countries combined, although the population of that country is less than one fifth of the total Arab population.)

The position of individual incomes is weak and has been declining (UNDP 2002: 88):

Real per capita income for the period 1975–1998 as a whole grew very slowly, by around 0.5 per cent a year—in effect, a situation of quasi-stagnation. Meanwhile, the global average increase was more than 1.3 per cent a year, implying a relative deterioration in the average standard of living in the Arab region compared to the rest of the world.

This is also seen in measures of "purchasing power parity" (UNDP 2002: 89):

In 1975, real PPP GDP per capita in the Arab world . . . was 21.3 per cent . . . one fifth of the OECD level. By 1998, the real PPP income of the average Arab citizen had fallen to 13.9 per cent, or one seventh, of that of the average OECD citizen.

Not addressed in this report is how much of the income of Arab countries is derived from oil, a product discovered by Westerners, processed by Western technology, used for Western technology, and paid for by Western and increasingly Asian consumers. Aside from oil, many Arab countries have precious little production to rely on.

As anticipated by the assessment of a "freedom deficit" in the Arab region, there is little encouragement to be found in governance (UNDP 2002: 108):

Political participation is less advanced in the Arab world than in other developing regions. In many countries of Latin America, East and South-East Asia, and sub-Saharan Africa, freedom of association is less restricted, governments change through the ballot box and people's groups have been encouraged to express themselves in various ways.

Governmental institutions in the Arab world—judged on the areas of quality, graft, rule of law, regulatory burden, effective-

ness, political instability, and voice and accountability—fall
below the world average (UNDP 2002: 111–12).

Combining indices for freedom, institutional features, and
human development for a general assessment of welfare produces a somewhat discouraging assessment for Arab countries
(UNDP 2002: 113):

> No Arab country enjoys high human welfare. Seven Arab
> countries, representing only 8.9 per cent of the population
> of the sample of 17, enjoy medium human welfare. The
> remaining 10 Arab countries, accounting for 91.1 per cent of
> the sample population, have low human welfare.

This result is disappointing, but not surprising, given the low
scores on economics, governance, education, and knowledge.

Statistical comparisons are a useful kind of knowledge, but
they are cold. The facts presented above reflect millions of human
faces, human worries, and human sentiments. Some are driven to
anger and despair. I shall quote only one. The poet Nizar Qabbani
came to the conclusion in 1985, at the height of the destruction of
Beirut, that he could no longer write (Ajami 1999: 112):

> I don't write because I can't say something that equals the
> sorrow of this Arab nation. I can't open any of the countless
> dungeons in this large prison. The poet is made of flesh and
> blood: you can't make him speak when he loses his appetite
> for words: you can't ask him to entertain and enthrall when
> there is nothing in the Arab world that entertains or
> enthralls. When we were secondary schoolchildren our his-
> tory teacher used to call the Ottoman empire "the sick man."
> What is the history teacher to call these mini-empires of the
> Arab world being devoured by disease? What are we to call
> these mini-empires with broken doors and shattered win-
> dows and blown-away roofs? What can the writer say and
> write in this large Arab hospital?

CONCLUSION

The countries of the Arab Middle East do not function well. In governance, economics, science, education, and welfare, they tend to score at the bottom in comparison with countries of other regions. Worse, their performance is declining relative to other countries that are developing impressively.

In historical perspective this is shocking, for the Islamic Middle East, including the Arab countries and Ottoman Turkey, dominated for over a thousand years much of the known world, from the Atlantic, around most of the Mediterranean, through the Middle East, and into India. Only in the last few centuries did Europe gain ascendancy (McNeill 1963). Although some of the accoutrements of Western modernization were adopted, only in the geographically reduced Republic of Turkey under Mustafa Kemal Ataturk was the fundamental structure of society modernized.

The Arab Middle East has remained largely a premodern, traditional society, based on subsistence economics, knowledge rooted in religion, social ties based on group affiliations, relations defined by balanced opposition, resorting to violence to resolve conflicts, and governance by coercion. This is partly due precisely to the historical dominance of the Arabs, whose pride in being the first Muslims and the fathers of the Islamic *umma* (community) and *dar al Islam* (the land of Islam), and in having conquered the world, remains and engenders a sense of superiority. After all, if one is superior, why change?

It is true that there were brief European imperial and colonial disruptions in the Middle East, and that Arab leaders chose European national socialism and Russian socialism as models for modernization: These have come and gone, they have been largely overlayers added to, but they have not replaced traditional tribal society based on group affiliation and balanced opposition. It is to the latter that we must look to understand the current circumstances and difficulties of the Arab Middle East. The lesson is that, in the Arab world and elsewhere, culture matters.

Chapter 7

ROOT CAUSES

The Middle East Today and Tomorrow

W hat underlies the characteristics and the difficulties of the central Middle East, both in the past and in the contemporary world? What are the root causes of the Middle East as we know it?

It will come as no surprise that there are markedly differing views on this matter. Assessments of the underlying causes of Middle Eastern patterns of life and events are highly contested, as we like to say today. It is illuminating to explore the various views, and to see where our thesis about the importance of balanced opposition fits.

THE CONTRADICTION BETWEEN THE STATE AND THE TRIBES

Ibn Khaldun sees Middle Eastern society as fundamentally mal-integrated. On the one hand, there is the state apparatus:

the ruler, his court, his regional representatives, his army, and his dependent regional populations are the main elements. On the other hand, there are the tribes: located in the desert and mountain peripheries, they consist of solidary groups of kinsmen who value independence and are disinclined to take orders or pay taxes.

The state and the tribes are an unstable mix. Sovereignty and suzerainty are contested among them. State leaders are often on the defensive, trying to hold together their realm in spite of the weak solidarity among them. Tribes, in contrast, watch and wait for their opportunity, not only to assert their full independence, but to step in and capture the state for themselves. Here is Khaldun's political cycle: Hardy, bellicose tribesmen from the periphery, enjoying strong kin solidarity among themselves, conquer a weak state and its sedentary urbanites and villagers, and set themselves up as rulers. They divide up the country among themselves, but in doing so divide themselves among the country. Acting as rulers and members of court, and as regional governors and officials, they enjoy the fruits of the rich urban and agricultural environment, and into this environment their children are born. The tribal hardiness and kin solidarity dissipate over generations, if not sooner. Now they have become the weak state. And they are being watched from the periphery by hardy, bellicose tribesmen waiting for their chance to snatch the prize for themselves.

Geertz's analysis illuminates Khaldun's formulation by specifying rulers' strategies in this delicate balance of state and tribe. At the top of the ruler's priorities must be cementing relations with tribal groups and discouraging adventurism. He does this by constant travel and visits to tribal regions with his impressive entourage to persuade tribesmen of his worthiness as leader and his steadfastness against any challenge. These deadly serious royal parades take place within a general, agonistic cultural milieu, in which, at all levels, each and every relationship, engagement, and transaction is a struggle between the parties. It would not be too much of an exaggeration to say that, in these circumstances, might makes fight, and the winner is always right.

Balanced opposition is not seen here only in the formal structure of tribes, but more broadly in society, throughout the range of social transactions. At the maximal level, the state apparatus is balanced against the weight of the surrounding tribes, and is constantly trying to keep its balance. Where balanced opposition is not found is between the state apparatus and its full dependents, the urbanites and peasant villagers whose meager power cannot claim respect, and who serve as resources to be exploited by the state. Otherwise, the spirit of agonism, of balanced opposition, dominates.

THE VIRTUES OF ARAB CULTURE: TO A FAULT

Many of the qualities that the modern West prides itself on are also found at the heart of Arab culture. This is the thesis of the magistral overview of the Muslim Middle East offered by Charles Lindholm (2002: 13).

> The Middle East has at its core many of the values that are presently believed to be essential characteristics of the modern western world: egalitarianism, individualism, pluralism, competitiveness, calculating rationality, personal initiative, social mobility, freedom; but these are set within a distinctive historical [or, we might say, cultural] context based upon chivalric honor, female seclusion, and patrilineality and that also favored invidious distinctions between men and women, whites and blacks, tribesmen and peasants, nobles and commoners, freemen and slaves [and particularly between Muslims and infidels].

The historical setting in which this culture developed was the one described by Ibn Khaldun. In Lindholm's (2002: 259) words,

> The cultural heritage of the Middle East . . . is structured by an ancient antagonism between unstable urban civilizations and armed peripheries. This fluid and unreliable setting has favored an entrepreneurial ethic of risk-taking, individual initiative, adaptiveness and mobility among opportunistic co-equals who struggle over ephemeral positions of power and respect, constrained only by participation in a framework of elastic patrilineages.

The problem that arises in Lindholm's review, which includes brief historical accounts of the alternation between despotisms and rebellions, is the ongoing difficulty of establishing a stable and peaceful society. In this, the Arabs differed from the Turks and Persians, who with cultures more congenial to authority, were more successful at supporting societal political structures. The nub of the problem, according to Lindholm (2002: 262, 269), is that the virtues of equality and autonomy are taken to a fault, denying a legitimate basis for authority in leadership and hierarchical political structures, for in Arab culture, "Deference is humiliating, to whomever one defers, and all yokes, however light, are too heavy to bear with honor."

> Competitive egalitarian individualism has an inherent dilemma—that is, how to conceptualize the actual relations of hierarchy and command that must exist in any complex social formation. In Middle Eastern secular politics the answer to this question has been simple. As Fredrik Barth writes: "It is the fact of effective control and ascendancy—not its formal confirmation or justification—that is consistently pursued." For the leader, and for his subjects, political domination in itself was unambiguously seen as a goal to be achieved simply

because power obliged the deference of others and thereby affirmed the ruler's personal strength and glory.

The other side of power is compliance. According to Lindholm (2002: 262),

> Compliance in the Middle East therefore has very often been a direct result of fear, since otherwise a man would not willingly obey another man who is, in principle, no better than he is.

But power is not absolute and so neither is compliance (Lindholm 2002: 262):

> The state is popularly understood, in Clifford Geertz's words, as a "machine less for the governing of men . . . than for the amassment and consumption of the material rewards of power." . . .
>   . . . Ruling by pure force, no secular leader can credibly claim any intrinsic right to the wealth or power he manages to accumulate; as a result, his position can be continually and convincingly challenged by new claimants.

The Arab secular rulers and the state, based on power alone and designed for the benefit and glory of the rulers, are seen among Arabs commonly as illegitimate and unjust. Reaction, often violent rebellion, has frequently taken the form of a religiously inspired holy war against the godless secular ruler. In the name of Islam, a vision of a just, religious government guides popular insurgency and rebel leaders (Lindholm 2002: 268–71). Many religious figures have thus been catapulted into power. Regrettably, this expedient fails to provide a satisfactory resolution of the dilemma of equality and autonomy vs. legitimate authority, for, as has happened repeatedly in the past, "Any claims to sacred authority are bound to be rendered questionable by the exigencies of secular power, and political failures must lead to an even greater disillusionment with government among the faithful" (Lindholm 2002: 271). This process, I would add, we see exactly as Lindholm formulates it, in Iran, where disillusionment with the clergy is widespread among the populace. The result of these considerations is that Lindholm ends on a discouraging note, citing contradictions between Arab cultural values of equality and autonomy, on the one hand, and legitimate authority, on the other, to explain the tyranny, disorder, and violence that has so often characterized the Arab body politic.

THE MISSING CONSTITUTION

If a cultural commitment to equality, autonomy, pluralism, initiative, and competitiveness is not sufficient in the Arab Middle East for engendering societal stability and a legitimate polity, what is the missing ingredient? What glue binds these elements into a stable whole, a functional, legitimate polity? Huntington (1996), in his controversial masterwork, *The Clash of Civilizations and the Remaking of World Order*, addresses exactly this question, and proposes an answer.

However, in proposing his answer, Huntington (1996: 311, see also 69–72, 305), stresses the unique culture of the West and its contrast with other cultures and civilizations.

> The West differs from other civilizations not in the way it has developed but in the distinctive character of its values and institutions. These include most notably its Christianity, pluralism, individualism, and rule of law. . . . In their ensemble these characteristics are peculiar to the West. Europe, as Arthur M. Schlesinger, Jr., has said, is "the source—the *unique* source" of the "ideas of individual liberty, political democ-

racy, the rule of law, human rights, and cultural freedom. . . . These are *European* ideas, not Asian, nor African, nor Middle Eastern ideas, except by adoption." They make Western civilization unique, and Western civilization is valuable not because it is universal but because it *is* unique.

Huntington here is stressing the differences among civilizations, while Lindholm was emphasizing commonalities between the Muslim Middle East and the West. To repeat, the elements that Lindholm (2002: 13) argues as commonalities are "egalitarianism, individualism, pluralism, competitiveness, calculating rationality, personal initiative, social mobility, freedom." The element of Huntington (1996: 70, see also 305) absent from this list, leaving aside Christianity, is "the rule of law."

> The concept of the centrality of law to civilized existence was inherited from the Romans. Medieval thinkers elaborated the idea of natural law according to which monarchs were supposed to exercise their power, and a common law tradition developed in England. . . . The tradition of rule of law laid the basis for constitutionalism and the protection of human rights, including property rights, against the exercise of arbitrary power. In most other civilizations law was a much less important factor in shaping thought and behavior.

In the Arab Middle East, the rule of law has not been a dominant or even evident factor in the establishment of public order and political control. As has been described in detail in earlier chapters, at the local and regional levels, tribal organization dominates; in the urban centers and at the national level, coercive power from the top down is characteristic. Nor has Islamic law provided the constitutionalism to bind society and provide order through constraint. How can this absence of the rule of law and of constitutionalism in the Middle East be explained?

BALANCED OPPOSITION AS A STRUCTURAL DETERMINANT

In the Arab world, embedded in social relations at every level, is balanced opposition, as I have argued in earlier chapters. It would not be unreasonable to say that balanced opposition is the most basic *modus operandi* in Arab social and political action. Balanced opposition is more than a value, it is the very structure of social relations. I would venture to say that it is taken for granted by people, thought of, to the extent that it can be thought of, as "natural" and "inevitable." It would be extremely difficult for Middle Easterners to step back and look critically at balanced opposition, just as any underlying principle of culture is difficult for a member of that culture to become conscious of and imagine alternatives to.

The observations of Ibn Khaldun, Lindholm, and Huntington set out above can be illuminated by considering them in the light of our thesis about the importance of balanced opposition. Ibn Khaldun stresses, as we have described, the *asabiyya*, or solidarity, ascribed to kin groups among the tribes. Anthropological research on tribal structure suggests that this kin group solidarity is rooted not only in the concept of descent as Ibn Khaldun suggests, but also in the balanced opposition provided by structurally equivalent kin groups of parallel descent. That outside opposition stimulates internal cohesion in groups has long been discussed in sociology (Simmel 1955; Coser 1956, 1967). That the opposition is not only instrumental and opportunistic, but also structural and continuous, guarantees a high level of solidarity and mutual support.

Lindholm stresses the Arab ideology of equality, with its tenet of honor, as an explanation of the illegitimacy of political ascendancy. But how does this concept of equality arise and become so strongly cathected? The answer, I would suggest, is in the structure of balanced opposition, for here, among tribesmen, safety and security is guaranteed only by equivalent complementarity of balanced groups. Any dominance on the side of one party undermines safety and security on the side of the other party. The notion of honor is the cultural persuader of individuals in favor of acting for the group rather than for their own individual interests, and in favor of the long run rather than the immediate future. A tribesman looking to his individual and short-term interests would not put himself at risk for an injury to some distant relative; but the certainty of losing his honor, and thus reputation and standing, persuades him to step forward in the group interest. In the Arab world, opposition is an ingrained structure of organization and action, fueled at the individual level by "honor."

Huntington's "rule of law" and "constitutionalism" have not existed in the Arab Middle East because among Arabs the primary and exclusive commitment is to the group, rather than to any abstract, universally applicable rules. The frame of reference is always "my group vs. the other group." The ultimate goal is never following a rule, but winning, or at least not losing. In this way, balanced opposition is a structural alternative to "the rule of law" and "constitutionalism." Islam, which conceivably could provide such an overarching constitution of universalistic rules binding together all members of society, was in fact built on a foundation of structural balanced opposition, and reflects that structure in its fierce oppositions, such as those between Sunni vs. Shiite—a split, in the spirit of balanced opposition, founded on adherence to two different lines of closely related relatives from Mecca (Lindholm 2002: 99, chart 6.2)—and between Muslim vs. infidel.

Balanced opposition thus makes an inclusive, integrated polity virtually impossible. Fragmentation is inherent in the most basic organizational principle in Arab Middle Eastern society. Group loyalty always trumps abstract rules, and oppositional splits always trump societal unity. With a structural foundation of balanced opposition, there is no basis in the

Arab Middle East for constitutionalism. Whatever formal unity and practical quietism may for a period exist is imposed by coercive force—we need only think of the regimes in Saudi Arabia, Syria, Iraq, Egypt, Libya, Tunisia, Algeria, Morocco, and so on—and remains illegitimate in the eyes of the subjects on the receiving end, and thus constantly open to violent challenge and radical replacement. The primary goal of such regimes is to remain in power and maximize spoils, rather than to enhance the lives of society members. Thus these societies perform poorly by most social, cultural, economic, and political criteria.

CULTURE AND EXPLANATION

In our quest to understand the contemporary central Middle East, we have identified a particular social structural characteristic, the principle of balanced opposition, to explain both the historical strengths and contemporary difficulties of Arab societies. In this exercise, we have worked at a high level of abstraction, considering Arab society in general, with little attention to the real variations among different Arab societies, in much the same way that a biologist could discuss the nature of camels in comparison with other species, without distinguishing between the very different slim, one-hump, hot weather dromedary and the heavy, wooly, two-hump, cold weather Bactrian varieties.

Central Middle Eastern societies share certain characteristics in spite of their differences, just as camels of different varieties share certain characteristics. Thus possible objections to our thesis based upon accusations of "essentialism" and "reductionism"—the identification of some characteristics to the neglect of others, and the neglect of internal variety—would be misplaced, for all thinking requires abstraction and generalization. The serious question is whether a generalization is appropriate for the task undertaken, not whether it is appropriate for every conceivable issue. For our purposes, we have tried to identify major features of Arab Middle Eastern society that distinguish it from Euro-American, South Asian, and East Asian societies. For this purpose, it is clear that structural balanced opposition is a feature of great importance in the Arab world, and minor or nonexistent in the other cultural worlds.

We have identified balanced opposition in the Middle East as a form of organization with strengths and benefits and also with limitations. Its strengths include advancing security through group membership and deterrence against attack, as well as the ability to amass allies in opposition to structurally more distant foes. It was this structural ability to consolidate that led to the successful expansion of the Arab Empire through much of the known world. At the same time, the framing of relations in terms of balanced opposition inhibits inclusiveness and unity, and is inimical to defining relations in terms of universally applied rule of law and constitutionalism.

Our observations of the limitations of balanced opposition and the detrimental effects on contemporary Arab societies take us into a controversial area. In general, anthropologists disdain criticizing or pointing out shortcomings or limitations among the peoples they study; they tend to hold to the principle, "If you cannot say anything good, don't say anything at all." Second, many writers identifying themselves as adherents to "postcolonial theory" have made careers accusing Euro-American researchers on the Middle East of spinning derogatory fantasies and myths about the Middle East, the purpose of which allegedly is to justify Euro-American imperialism and colonialism in the Middle East. This tendentious argument, advanced vigorously by advocates of various Middle Eastern political causes, negates both the possibility of knowledge in general and the fact-based understanding of the Middle East. Postcolonialists argue that it is futile to study the nature of the Middle East, because Middle Eastern society and culture, and any problems or difficulties found in that region, have arisen from Euro-American imperialism and colonialism rather than from any fundamental characteristics of the societies themselves.

As far as this volume is concerned, my intention is to present a realistic, fact-based account of central elements of Arab culture and their impact on Arab society. Both strengths and limitations have been presented in what might fairly be called a balanced account. As regards postcolonial theory, the position of postcolonialist theorists is refuted on three grounds: First, the anthropologists who have lived and carried out ethnographic field research in the Middle East have been invariably sympathetic to the people whom they have studied, and have criticized external interference. Their descriptions and analyses of Arab culture and society are meant to do honor to the subjects of their study, and any limitation or possible weakness described is simply adherence to the ethnographic facts. Second, the characteristics of Arab Middle Eastern society are of long standing, while European and American incursions in the Middle East are quite recent and of short duration. During the thousand and more years of Arab and Islamic expansion, dominance, empire, and colonialism, the social and cultural features described, particularly tribal balanced opposition and its constraints on inclusiveness and unity, were constantly in evidence. Third, the weaknesses and flaws of contemporary central Middle Eastern societies have been cataloged in detail by accredited Arab scholars and observers, international bodies, and other non-Euro-American parties. Members of these societies themselves are commonly strong critics of their societies' shortcomings.

PROSPECTS FOR CHANGE

A major contemporary current of thought about the Arab Middle East argues that the major factor inhibiting social and economic development, and civil peace, is the absence of democracy, and that the missing ingredient is the electoral accountability of the governments of Arab societies (Sharansky 2004). There is much to be said for this view, but we would want to add that successful electoral politics presumes—requires as a prerequisite—the rule of law and constitutionalism. Democracy only works when all parties are committed to the electoral rules and are prepared to defer to the results of the polls. Otherwise, election results become an occasion for a standoff between opponent parties and a rebellion by the unelected party. Equally, a violation of democracy is the permanent monopolization of power by a once-elected party: one man, one vote, one time.

The culture of balanced opposition precludes democracy by its unwavering commitment to group loyalty and interests, and its disregard for other groups and their interests, and for any inclusive framework and process. The Sunni minority in Iraq and the Alawite minority in Syria provide outstanding examples of groups happy to use any means to maintain ascendancy over majority populations. But as well the general commitment to kin, tribal, ethnic, and religious groups throughout the Arab Middle East, the reliance on them for support and protection, and the framing of these memberships in terms of loyalty and honor, is a monumental inhibition to the development of universal citizenship and functional democracy, and the rule of law and constitutionalism upon which they rest.

What is necessary for shifting away from group loyalty and balanced opposition is individualization, in which political and legal standing is given to individuals rather than groups.

The possibility of inclusive unity in Arab society is contingent upon the delegitimization of the traditional divisive groupings. This is possible not through the replacement of traditional groups with newly conceived groups, but by the replacement of groups by individuals. It may seem anachronistic to advocate individualism, just as Western countries are jettisoning their individualist traditions and universalistic standards, and granting collective rights and special privileges to particular groups and categories, justified in terms of multiculturalism. But Western civil society was built on the principles of individualism and universalism, and its strengths are derived from those principles. Current faddish policies of collectivism and special privileges may well eventually undermine those traditional strengths of Western society. However, recommendations for building an inclusive and unified civil society in the Middle East would focus on those foundational principles, individualism and universalism, for it is on them that Western rule of law and constitutionalism were based.

CONCLUSION

Basic principles of tribal organization have become central cultural principles of Middle Eastern life. Most important are two working in tandem: *balanced opposition* (each group of whatever size and scope is opposed by a group of equal size and scope) and *affiliation solidarity* (always support those closer against those more distant). Success in competition, conflict, and combat brings *honor*, while defeat brings loss of honor and *shame*.

The consequences of these ingenious structural principles are pervasive and determining: On the positive side, balanced opposition and affiliation solidarity support a decentralized social and political system based upon individual independence, autonomy, liberty, equality, and responsibility. On the negative side, because each man is responsible for defense and security, martial arts are necessary and encouraged, and—most critical—*loyalty is always defined as support of one's own group in opposition to another group.*

This pattern of contingent partisan loyalties is dominant in Middle Eastern cultures, especially in the Arab Middle East. The result is an inbred orientation favoring *particularism*, support based upon particular affiliation: as the Arab saying puts it, I against my brother; I and my brothers against my cousins; I and my brothers and my cousins against the world. The morality of this particularism directs each to try to advantage his group and disadvantage opposing groups: my family against their family; my lineage against that lineage; my tribe against the other tribe; my ethnic group against the different ethnic group; my religious community against another religious community. For each affiliation, there is always an enemy. For each act, the important questions are who acted, who was affected, and who is closest to me?

The particularism of Middle Eastern culture precludes *universalism*, *rule of law*, and *constitutionalism*, all involving the measuring of actions against general criteria, irrespective of the affiliation of the particular actors. What is right and wrong is defined under rule of law and constitutionalism by general values that apply to all, not by whether one or one's group is advantaged or disadvantaged.

Middle Eastern society has in modern times suffered from the pervasive particularism enjoined by its culture. Apparently unending conflict, both internal and external, results from this relentless partisan framework of thought. The reason that modern Middle Eastern societies have been uniformly unproductive, oppressive, and full of conflict is due in large part to their particularist cultural orientation. The contrast in productivity and human rights with Euro-American and Asian societies with universalist orientations is very marked indeed. To improve the condition of their society, Middle Easterners will have to decide that *what they are for* is more important than *whom they are against*.

REFERENCES

2005. "Al-Qaeda Captures Iraqi Governor." *National Post* (May 11), p. A12.

2005. "New King Vows to 'Hear and Obey.'" *Ottawa Citizen* (August 4), p. A8.

2005. "Voices of Hatred." *National Post* (May 17), p. A16.

2006. "Gaza Clashes Threaten Ceasefire." *Ottawa Citizen* (December 22), p. A12.

2006. "They Never Saw Each Other as an Enemy." *Globe and Mail* (Canada) (December 21).

Abedin, Mahan. 2005. "The Heart of Sunni Rage." *National Post* (May 14), p. A19.

Abou-Zeid, A. M. 1959. "The Sedentarization of Nomads in the Western Desert of Egypt." *International Social Science Journal* 11, no. 4: 550–58.

Abu-Rabia, Aref. 1994. *The Negev Bedouin and Livestock Rearing.* Oxford: Berg.

Ahmed, Akbar S. 1980. *Pakhtun Economy and Society.* London: Routledge & Kegan Paul.

Ajami, Fouad. 1999. *The Dream Palace of the Arabs.* New York: Vintage.

Al-Halyan, Eissa. 2004. "Improving Arab Universities." *National Post* (November 24), p. A19. Originally published in the Saudi daily *Al-Jazirah*, translated by the Middle East Media Research Institute.

Arfa, Hassan. 1964. *Under Five Shahs.* London: John Murray.

Avery, Peter. 1965. *Modern Iran.* London: Ernest Benn Ltd.

Barth, Fredrik. 1953. *Principles of Social Organization in Southern Kurdistan.* Universitets Etnografiske Museum Bulletin 7. Oslo: Brodrene Jorgensen A/S.

———. 1961. *Nomads of South Persia.* Oslo: Oslo University Press.

———. 1983. *Sohar: Culture and Society in an Omani Town.* Baltimore: Johns Hopkins University Press.

Bat Ye'or (see Ye'or, Bat).

Bates, Daniel G. 1973. *Nomads and Farmers: A Study of the Yoruk of Southeastern Turkey.* Anthropological Papers, No. 52. Ann Arbor: University of Michigan Museum of Anthropology.

Beck, Lois. 1986. *The Qashqa'i of Iran.* New Haven, CT: Yale University Press.

———. 1991. *Nomad: A Year in the Life of a Qashqa'i Tribesman in Iran.* Berkeley: University of California Press.

Beeston, Richard. 2003. "'We Are Fighting for Honour,' Not Saddam." *Ottawa Citizen* (December 15), p. A9.

Ben-Meir, Alon. 2005. "Iraq's Insurgency—A Catch 22." February 27. www.alonben-meir.com.

Bostom, Andrew G., ed. 2005. *The Legacy of Jihad: Islamic Holy War and the Fate of Non-Muslims.* Amherst, NY: Prometheus Books.

Bujra, Abdalla. 1971. *The Politics of Stratification: A Study of Political Change in a South Arabian Town.* Oxford: Clarendon Press.

Campbell, J. K. 1964. *Honour, Family and Patronage.* Oxford: Clarendon Press.

Chatty, Dawn. 1996. *Mobile Pastoralists: Development Planning and Social Change in Oman.* New York: Columbia University Press.

Cohen, Abner. 1965. *Arab Border-Villages in Israel.* Manchester: Manchester University Press.

Cole, Donald Powell. 1975. *Nomads of the Nomads: The Al Murrah Bedouin of the Empty Quarter.* Chicago: Aldine.

Cole, Donald Powell and Soraya Altorki. 1998. *Bedouin, Settlers, and Holiday-Makers: Egypt's Changing Northwest Coast.* Cairo: American University in Cairo Press.

Combs-Schilling, M. E. 1989. *Sacred Performances: Islam, Sexuality, and Sacrifice.* New York: Columbia University Press.

Cook, David. 2005. *Understanding Jihad.* Berkeley: University of California Press.

Coser, Lewis A. 1956. *The Functions of Social Conflict.* Glencoe, IL: Free Press.

———. 1967. *Continuities in the Study of Social Conflict.* New York: The Free Press.

Davis, Douglas. 2005. "Boycotting Israel? Read This." *National Post* (April 21), p. A16.

Davis, John. 1987. *Libyan Politics: Tribe and Revolution.* London: I. B. Tauris.

Evans-Pritchard, E. E. 1940. *The Nuer.* Oxford: Clarendon Press.

———. 1949. *The Sanusi of Cyrenaica.* Oxford: Clarendon Press.

Fallers, L. A. 1973. *Inequality: Social Stratification Reconsidered.* Chicago: University of Chicago Press.

Fisher, W. B., ed. 1968. *The Cambridge History of Iran: Volume I, The Land of Iran.* Cambridge: Cambridge University Press.

Garthwaite, Gene. 1983(a). "Tribes, Confederation and the State: An Historical Overview of the Bakhtairi and Iran." In Richard Trapper, ed., *The Conflict of Tribe and State in Iran.* London: Croom Helm.

———. 1983(b). *Khans and Shahs: A Documentary Analysis of the Bakhtiyari of Iran.* Cambridge: Cambridge University Press.

Geertz, Clifford. 1983. *Local Knowledge.* New York: Basic Books.

Geertz, Clifford, Hildred Geertz, and Lawrence Rosen. 1979. *Meaning and Order in Moroccan Society.* Cambridge: Cambridge University Press.

Gellner, Ernest. 1969. *Saints of the Atlas.* Chicago: University of Chicago Press.

———. 1981. *Muslim Society.* Cambridge: Cambridge University Press.

———. 1988. *Plough, Sword and Book: The Structure of Human History.* Chicago: University of Chicago Press.

Gellner, Ernest, and Charles Micaud, eds. 1973. *Arabs and Berbers: From Tribe to Nation in North Africa*. London: Duckworth.

Ginat, Joseph. 1997. *Blood Revenge: Family Honor, Mediation and Outcasting*. 2nd ed. Brighton: Sussex University Press.

Haddadin, Haitham. 2005. "Kuwait Grants Women Full Electoral Rights." *National Post* (17 May), p. A10.

Hart, David Montgomery. 1976. *The Aith Waryghar of the Moroccan Rif*. Viking Fund Publications in Anthropology, no. 55, Wenner Gren Foundation for Anthropological Research. Tucson: University of Arizona Press.

Hasan, Omar. 2005. "Kuwait Names Women to Join Civic Council." *National Post* (June 6), p. A11.

Heumann, Pierre. 2006. "An Interview with Al-Jazeera Editor in Chief Ahmed Sheikh." *World Politics Watch*. http://www.world politicswatch.com/article.aspx?id-395.

Hobbs, Joseph J. 1989. *Bedouin Life in the Egyptian Wilderness*. Austin: University of Texas Press.

Holt, P. M., Ann K. S. Lambton, and Bernard Lewis, eds. 1970. *The Cambridge History of Islam*. Cambridge: Cambridge University Press.

Huntington, Samuel P. 1996. *The Clash of Civilizations and the Remaking of World Order*. New York: Simon & Schuster.

Irons, William. 1965. "Livestock Raiding among Pastoralists: An Adaptive Interpretation." *Papers of the Michigan Academy of Science 50*.

———. 1975. *The Yomut Turkmen*. Anthropological papers no. 58. Ann Arbor: University of Michigan, Museum of Anthropology.

Kaplan, Robert D. 2007. "It's the Tribes, Stupid!" http://theatlantic .com/doc/2007llu/kaplan-democracy.

Karsh, Efraim. 2006. *Islamic Imperialism*. New Haven, CT: Yale University Press.

Khaldun, Ibn. 1967. *The Muqaddimah*. Princeton, NJ: Princeton University Press.

Kramer, Samuel Noah. 1963. *The Sumerians: Their History, Culture, and Character*. Chicago: University of Chicago Press.

Kressel, Gideon M. 1996. *Ascendancy through Aggression: The Anatomy of a Blood Feud among Urbanized Bedouins*. Wiesbaden: Harrassowitz.

————. 2003. *Let Shepherding Endure: Applied Anthropology and the Preservation of a Cultural Tradition in Israel and the Middle East.* Albany: State University of New York Press.

Lancaster, William. 1997. *The Rwala Bedouin Today.* 2nd ed. Prospect Heights, IL: Waveland.

Lancaster, William, and Fidelity Lancaster. 1999. *People, Land and Water in the Arab Middle East: Environments and Landscapes in the Bilâd ash-Shâm.* Amsterdam: Harwood Academic Publishers.

Lee, Richard Borshay. 1979. *The !Kung San: Men, Women, and Work in a Foraging Society.* Cambridge: Cambridge University Press.

————. 1993. *The Dobe Ju/'hoansi.* 2nd ed. Fort Worth: Harcourt Brace College Publishers.

Lewis, I. M. 1961. *A Pastoral Democracy: A Study of Pastoralism and Politics among the Northern Somali of the Horn of Africa.* London: Oxford University Press.

Lindholm, Charles. 2002. *The Islamic Middle East.* Rev. ed. Oxford: Blackwell Publishing.

Littman, David G., and Bat Ye'or. 2005. "Protected Peoples under Islam." In Robert Spencer, ed., *The Myth of Islamic Tolerance.* Amherst, NY: Prometheus Books. Originally published in 1976.

Marx, Emanuel. 1967. *Bedouin of the Negev.* Manchester: Manchester University Press.

McNeill, William H. 1963. *The Rise of the West.* Chicago: University of Chicago Press.

Meir, Avinoam. 1996. *As Nomadism Ends: The Israeli Bedouin of the Negev.* Boulder, CO: Westview.

Oppenheim, A. Leo. 1965. *Ancient Mesopotamia.* Chicago: University of Chicago Press.

Parsons, Talcott. 1954. *Essays in Sociological Theory.* Glencoe, IL: Free Press.

Peters, Emrys L. 1960. "The Proliferation of Segments in the Lineages of the Bedouin in Cyrenaica." *Journal of the Royal Anthropological Institute* 110: 29–53. Reprinted in Emrys L. Peters, *The Bedouin of Cyrenaica,* 1990, pp. 84–111.

————. 1967. "Some Structural Aspects of the Feud among the Camel-Herding Bedouin of Cyrenaica." *Africa* 35: 261–81. Reprinted in *The Bedouin of Cyrenaica,* 1990, pp. 59–83.

————. 1968. "The Tied and the Free: An Account of a Type of Patron–Client Relationship among the Bedouin Pastoralists of Cyrenaica." In J. G. Peristiany, ed., *Contributions to Mediterranean Sociology*. Paris and The Hague: Mouton, pp. 167–88. Reprinted in *The Bedouin of Cyrenaica*, 1990, pp. 40–58.

————. 1990. *The Bedouin of Cyrenaica: Studies in Personal and Corporate Power*. Cambridge: Cambridge University Press.

Pigliaru, Antonio. 1975. *Il banditismo in Sardegna: La vendetta barbaricina*. Nuova ed. Milano: Guiffré editore.

Sahlins, Marshall. 1961. "The Segmentary Lineage: An Organization of Predatory Expansion." *American Anthropologist* 63: 322–43.

Said, Edward W. 1978. *Orientalism*. New York: Random House.

Salzman, Philip Carl. 1978. "The Proto-State in Iranian Baluchistan." In *Origins of the State: The Anthropology of Political Evolution*, Ronald Cohen and Elman R. Service, eds. Philadelphia: Institute for the Study of Human Issues, pp. 125–40.

————. 1999. *The Anthropology of Real Life: Events in Human Experience*. Prospect Heights, IL: Waveland.

————. 2000. *Black Tents of the Baluchistan*. Washington: Smithsonian Institution Press.

————. 2004. *Pastoralists: Equality, Hierarchy, and the State*. Boulder: Westview Press.

Sharansky, Natan. 2004. *The Case for Democracy: The Power of Freedom to Overcome Tyranny and Terror*. New York: Public Affairs.

Simmel, Georg. 1955. *Conflict and the Web of Group-Affiliations*. Glencoe, IL: Free Press.

Spiro, Melford. 1973. "Social Change and Functional Analysis: A Study in Burmese Psychocultural History." *Ethos* 1, no. 3: 263–97.

Stewart, Frank Henderson. 1994. *Honor*. Chicago: University of Chicago Press.

Sweet, Louise. 1965. "Camel Raiding of North Arabian Bedouin: A Mechanism of Ecological Adaptation." *American Anthropologist* 67: 1132–50.

Trigger, Bruce. 2003. *Understanding Early Civilizations: A Comparative Study*. Cambridge: Cambridge University Press.

United Nations Development Program (UNDP), and the Arab Fund for Economic and Social Development. 2002. *Arab Human Development Report 2002*. New York: UNDP.

Ye'or, Bat. 2002. *Islam and Dhimmitude: Where Civilizations Collide*. Madison, NJ: Fairleigh Dickinson University Press.

Youssef, Nancy A., and Yasser Salihee. 2005. "Newly Elected Official Kidnapped." *Ottawa Citizen* (May 11), p. A11.

INDEX

ownership of the world, 148–49
tolerance, myth of, 152–58
tribal basis, 14
umma (community of Muslims),
    14
united tribes, 137–38
Israel, 180
    Arab attitudes toward, 160–61,
        163
    Arab attitudes, reasons for,
        163–70
    positive characteristics of,
        162–63

Jews, degradation of, 153–58
Jordan, 180, 185

Khaldun, Ibn, 52, 197–98, 204
Kressel, Gideon, 107
Kuwait, 179

Lewis, Bernard, 153
Libya, 179, 185. *See also* Cyrenaica
Lindholm, Charles, 139, 199–202,
    204
lineage organization
    descent, 67–68
    division, 39
    genealogy, 93
    group loyalty, 16
    inconsistent with universalism,
        16
    size and prestige, 112–14,
        128–29
    strategies for increasing size,
        114–15

Maghreb, North Africa, 61–63
mediation, 34, 80–81, 95–97, 109

migrant labor, 28
military
    capability and prowess, 15, 16
    Morocco, 180, 185
    motivation, 102
    in Middle East, 102–104
    political, 125–27

Nile River valley, 22
nomads, 32, 36, 40–41
    differences from peasants, 30–40
    settled by force, 42–43
nomadism, 25, 45
Nuer, 96

Oman, 179
"Other, the," 14
Ottoman Empire, 44–45. *See also*
    Cyrenaica; states

particularism, 16–17
pastoralism 25, 28, 30–31
    combined with other forms of
        production, 26–27
    livestock increase, 134–35
    production, 47–48
    tribal organization and, 35
peasants, 31–32, 39–40, 45–47
Persian crown. *See* states
politics. *See also* lineage organiza-
    tion; mediation; peasants;
    states; tribes
    domination, 16, 142, 145–46
    organization, 33
    religion, turn toward, 170–71
Postcolonial theory, 14–15, 187,
    207–208
    objections to, 15, 206–208
protection racket, 27